CHICAGO'S FAMOUS BUILDINGS

A PHOTOGRAPHIC GUIDE TO
THE CITY'S ARCHITECTURAL
LANDMARKS AND OTHER
NOTABLE BUILDINGS

CHICAGO'S FAMOUS BUILDINGS

Edited by ARTHUR SIEGEL

The University of Chicago Press

This book is also available in a clothbound edition from

THE UNIVERSITY OF CHICAGO PRESS

*Publication of this book was made possible
by generous grants from the Graham Foundation
for Advanced Studies in the Fine Arts
and from the City of Chicago*

Library of Congress Catalog Card Number: 64-15803

The University of Chicago Press, Chicago & London
The University of Toronto Press, Toronto 5, Canada

Foreword

BY IRA J. BACH

The Chicago School of Architecture is famous the world over, but visitors seeking out its best works have sometimes had difficulty locating them. Indeed, the people who live here have often been unaware of or unable to find the structures for which their city is so widely known. So the need for this book has been clear for some time.

In 1957 Mayor Richard J. Daley emphasized the need for preserving Chicago's architectural heritage by documentation and citation as well as actual preservation. He therefore recommended to the Chicago City Council that a commission be created to designate certain buildings as architectural landmarks. On the basis of an ordinance drafted by Alderman Leon Despres the Commission on Architectural Landmarks was organized, with seven members appointed by the Mayor and Daniel Catton Rich, then director of the Art Institute, as first chairman.

A committee of prominent architects and art historians was chosen to advise the Commission. After visiting many buildings that had been proposed as landmarks and after much deliberation, the Commission finally selected thirty-nine structures which met the criteria developed by the advisory committee and approved by the Commission. In a public ceremony Mayor Daley presented to the building owners distinctive plaques identifying the structures as architectural landmarks of Chicago. This means they are also to be considered landmarks in the history of modern architecture, for they constitute the most important innovations in the art of building since the Gothic cathedrals.

The ordinance creating the Commission directed that it "list and identify Chicago's architectural landmarks . . . [and] take steps to stimulate public interest in the identification and preservation of such landmarks." This directive made preparation of a guidebook an early project of the Commission.

The Commission solicited and received financial assistance from the Graham Foundation for Advanced Studies in the Fine Arts. A matching sum was received from the City of Chicago by action of the City Council upon recommendation of Mayor Daley.

Both the Commission and the Graham Foundation immediately agreed to expand the publication to include additional buildings. The advisory committee of the Commission was called in to serve once more and responded by recommending many more worthy buildings, some on the basis of architectural merit; others because they are considered to have a special symbolic, sentimental, or historic importance; a few for reasons of general interest. Meanwhile, Illinois Institute of Technology architectural students, under the direction of Dean George Danforth, measured and prepared plans of the architectural landmarks. Photography students of the Institute of Design of the Illinois Institute of Technology helped in photographing many of the buildings. The architectural firm of Skidmore, Owings and Merrill prepared the excellent maps. Arthur Siegel, who had already been responsible for supervising the photographic work by students and others, was appointed editor, and with his dedicated direction this book has been brought into final form.

Grateful thanks are due Mayor Richard J. Daley for his splendid co-operation with the Commission. His pride in Chicago and his appreciation for its exciting architectural history have been an inspiration.

The generosity of the Graham Foundation and its president, Charles F. Murphy, made the production of this guidebook possible. We are also grateful to John Entenza, director of the Foundation, for his professional assistance.

Commission Vice-Chairman Samuel A. Lichtmann headed the advisory committee and the guidebook committee. Our gratitude is offered to him and to his committees, as it is to Judge Augustine Bowe, who is Chairman of the Commission on Chicago Architectural Landmarks. Our thanks for the concise bibliography go to Miss Ruth Schoneman of the Burnham Library.

It is hoped that *Chicago's Famous Buildings* will assist not only the tourist to Chicago but also its citizens who take pride in their architectural heritage. It is hoped also that architects, engineers, planners, and students will use this book as a reference and for inspiration in their work.

IRA J. BACH

Commissioner of City Planning
Member of the Architectural
Landmarks Commission, 1964

Contents

Foreword *by Ira J. Bach*

The Chicago School: Principles . . .
by Hugh Dalziel Duncan / 1

The Chicago School: . . . and Practice
by Carl W. Condit / 13

Maps / 23

List of Buildings / 28

Photographic Guide: Descriptive Text
by Carson Webster / 41

Bibliography / 219

Glossary / 221

Credits / 224

Index of Buildings / 225

Index of Architects / 228

The Chicago School: Principles...

BY HUGH DALZIEL DUNCAN

The buildings illustrated in this guide are part of the great cultural heritage of America. Chicago is the national, and indeed the world, capital for historical landmarks of modern architecture. Almost the whole history of what we call "contemporary design" can be examined in Chicago. For Chicago is the birthplace of modern architecture, and some of the buildings illustrated here are among the first, and greatest, examples of it. That is why architects come from all over the world to study these great buildings. Chicago is the urban center of the life and work of Frank Lloyd Wright and Mies van der Rohe, who, along with Le Corbusier, are the great architects of our time. Another Chicagoan, Louis Henri Sullivan, was the master from whom Wright, Mies, and Le Corbusier drew inspiration in developing their talents and their understanding of the architect's role in society.

The architecture of the Chicago School was first considered a style among many styles. From 1890 until about 1920, it was thought of as commercial or industrial architecture. In the twenties, many critics dismissed the work of the Chicago School as representing a crude "commercial" style to be "refined" by other architects. Such architects, mostly classicists, were educated in European schools and worked with clients who were interested in beautiful buildings so long as the beauty was European, not American. Sullivan, it was admitted, had done some good ornament, but this was really wasted, and even "out of place," on commercial buildings. But in the thirties, as the work of Le Corbusier and

Perret in France, Behrens, Gropius, Mendelsohn, and Mies van der Rohe in Germany, Berlage and Dudok in Holland, and Frank Lloyd Wright in America began to be accepted as genuinely creative, even conventional critics were forced to admit that modern architecture might be more than a passing fad.

An order of architecture, unlike a style, expresses a way of life. It is the expression of the community, not simply that of a class or an individual. This community for Jenney, Adler, Root, Burnham, and Wright was the democratic community. For however the architects of the Chicago School differed on design and however they argued about the relationship of engineering and architecture, they all agreed that the only architecture worth having was a democratic architecture. Indeed, Sullivan taught that democracy *depended* on its architects as much as on its statesmen or businessmen. He argued, with deep and prophetic conviction, that until democracy produced a good architecture and good art, it could not produce a good life for its citizens. Thus from the very beginning modern architecture in Chicago was part of a search for a social philosophy of democracy, as well as a search for perfection of form.

But while it was easy enough to talk about a people's art and a democratic architecture, it was another matter to produce it. In both his buildings and his early talks to Chicagoans on architecture, Sullivan asked questions: What is the proper form for a democratic architecture, and what kinds of human relationships will be possible in this new architecture? He answered the first by proposing that whatever the use of a building, its form must follow its function—not a mechanical function, like a traffic flow, circulation of air, heating, lighting, etc., but *human* function. He thought that the architect must ask himself: How can I enhance the human satisfaction of acting within my building or the communities I design? If I design a house of prayer, how do I make prayer more significant? If I design a department store, how do I make shopping more pleasurable? If I design a factory, how do I make work healthy and pleasur-

2

able? If I design a tomb, how do I make the sorrowing family feel the serenity and peace of death as a memory of life?

This is what Sullivan meant by his constantly repeated phrase: "A building is an act." And it is also what he meant by insisting that a building, indeed all architecture, is a moral act because it is an aesthetic act. In his *Kindergarten Chats*, the record of the spiritual voyage of a young architect, Sullivan takes us on a walk through the streets of Chicago, his city of joy and sorrow. As we walk beside the master we discover that he reads buildings as we read character in the faces of people. Perhaps this is why he hated "phony" buildings. He thought a bank should look like a friendly meeting place for neighbors who had come to see each other and to talk over their problems with bank officials. A bank which looked like a fort, a great vault, a Roman temple, or a Gothic cathedral, enraged him. Why, he asked, does the banker not dress in a Roman toga and talk in Latin? And why, he asked over and over again, is the banker ashamed to be an American in his expression of a most characteristic American act—the exchange of money?

Nor would Sullivan agree to any hierarchy of content, or to the commonly accepted distinction between fine and applied art. Like Thorstein Veblen and Frank Lloyd Wright, who followed Sullivan's teaching, he argued that invention was the mother of necessity. What the engineer invented, or the artist created, became needs. That is, the people did not have needs which they "asked" the artist to satisfy, nor were there "social forces," like evolution or the class struggle, which determined the forms of architecture. The people and the artist *shared* problems. The true democratic artist accepted these problems as his problems, and tried to solve them through the creation of buildings and cities which would enhance the democratic qualities of human relationships. The democratic architect must create communities where *all* men could walk in dignity, freedom, and joy in human brotherhood.

Thus, in the development of the Burnham Plan for the city of Chicago, the problem of traffic, of the city as a community in motion, was faced in common by architects, engi-

3

neers, sociologists, economists, civic officials, and representatives of the people. The art involved in the creation of such a plan was certainly applied art, but it never occurred to Burnham that he should not use all the resources of fine art to create his plan. True, the purpose of any city plan was to insure a good flow of traffic, but Chicagoans did not want their traffic to flow right through or around the city. They wanted to make it easy for people to get in and out of the Loop, but they also wanted people to stop in their hotels, stores, and restaurants, and to find homes in the city. Burnham, Root, Sullivan, and Wright argued that people would stop only if the Loop, and the whole of the city, were interesting and beautiful. The first mark of beauty in architecture was the way in which it brought order into the human environment. A city was beautiful because it solved the problem (among others) of how to get automobiles and people through its streets, house and feed them during their stay in the city, and offer fit dwelling places for families.

Sullivan, and certainly Sullivan's great pupil, Wright, were as sensitive as Burnham to the need for planning. Wright warned Chicagoans at the time the original Chicago Plan was promoted that the future of our city would be a race between the elevator and the automobile, and he declared that wise Chicagoans would bet on the automobile. But Root, Sullivan, and Wright were more concerned than Burnham with the kinds of human satisfactions architecture could give people, the humble as well as the great, in their daily personal lives. They asked State Street merchants: What is the use of bringing people to the Loop unless our stores are exciting, our factories decent places to work, our hotels comfortable and luxurious, and our city a suitable environment for families?

Questions like these had been asked before, but few architects had asked them in relation to *all* the people of a community—a community where hundreds of thousands of people and millions of tons of goods must be moved with every turn of the clock. The great cities of the past, such as Rome, were planned for movement and the sheltering of huge crowds for special civic events, but never before in the history of the world had there been need to design for the swift movement of machines as well as people. And never before was a city designed by architects who asked themselves: How can I design for the greatest number of people and yet give each individual the greatest possible satisfaction? Thus, when Adler designed his great Auditorium, he approached acoustics as the art of distributing sound to the largest possible audience. He wanted the poorest student in the most remote section of the Auditorium, as well as the rich and mighty in their boxes, to hear. In hall after hall he tried to bring sound, in all its purity and beauty, to the people. His successes in the Auditorium and Carnegie Hall are now part of our national heritage.

In the same spirit, Sullivan designed the Schlesinger and Mayer Store (now the Carson Pirie Scott Store). Like the owners, he was eager to attract the largest number of people into the store, but, unlike the bankers and their architects, he did not want to attract customers through inspiring them with awe. He wanted to make shopping a joyful, exciting event, not for just a few rich customers, but for all the people. Nor did he think of the store as an imposing facade which could be used to lure people inside. Without and within it was to be a great bazaar whose tone of elegance, gaiety, and graciousness would give women of all ranks pleasure in their femininity and create a gracious stage for the spending of money in a tasteful and dignified manner.

Sullivan did not think of the Schlesinger and Mayer Store as a proud, soaring tower, thrusting up into the sky. He had designed and built such towers. But a store for women should not be a proud, arrogant tower. So he accentuated the horizontal plane, the human plane of man on earth, which Wright and Jensen used so often in their homes for Chicago families. Shopping should be gay and festive, the trip downtown a small adventure, and for women who were just beginning to appear in public without their men, stores must be a gracious retreat from the burly masculine tone of the street or the wholesale store which merely tolerated retail customers. Each floor must be a great but elegant stage filled with treasures from the four corners of the earth. Onto this stage

5

timid young immigrant women, middle-class wives seeking good buys, and the stately matrons of high society were invited. The floors of these great State Street stores became a great promenade, like the square of an ancient city, where all came to see—and to be seen. Here, for the first time, the "shawl trade" and the "carriage trade" met as audiences before each other.

The public schools designed by Dwight H. Perkins show this same spirit in education. Carl Schurz High School and Grover Cleveland Elementary School were designed to create a beautiful and serene experience for children and youths of all classes and races. They were in every sense people's schools. The sons and daughters of poor immigrants who went through these schools have told us what it meant to go from the squalor of poverty and ignorance to such buildings. For many, the hours spent in the school were their only experience of a decent habitation. As such students walked through the doors of these schools, the promise of democracy became real. In their public, if not in their private, lives, they could walk the earth with dignity as sons and daughters of a city whose civic leaders believed that *all* men should be decently clothed, housed, fed, and educated.

And nowhere does the profundity of the work of the Chicago School show more clearly than in Sullivan's Getty Tomb in Graceland Cemetery. In some ways this tomb, which Frank Lloyd Wright cherished so deeply, is Chicago's most profound utterance in democratic art. Beside the grandiose mausoleums of Chicago's great families from 1875 to 1910, the Carrie Eliza Getty Tomb stands in quiet simplicity. As Hugh Morrison says in his book *Louis Sullivan: Prophet of Modern Architecture:* "The sentiment expressed in the majority of monuments is the preoccupation with death, its awfulness, its inevitability, its utter permanence. . . . A different spirit animates Sullivan's tombs. They celebrate, not the permanence of death, but the permanence of life; they express in terms of lyric beauty that a man or woman has *lived*, not merely he or she has died." This is expressed, not in gold or marble, but in blocks of gray Bedford limestone

6

whose rich ornament is subordinated to architectural expression.

Outside of Chicago, few understood the significance of Chicago design. Adams, Norton, Bourget, and other visitors, during the years following the World's Columbian Exposition of 1893, told their readers and hearers that Chicago architecture, as indeed the whole city, was based on making money. And since the making of money, if not its possession, was, in the eyes of traditional aesthetes and the aristocracies of Europe and America, essentially an ignoble pursuit, how could culture, to say nothing of great art, come from business people? Easterners like Adams, Norton, Henry James, and Edith Wharton admitted that Chicago was "interesting" and even "significant," but its significance as a center of American art was simply beyond their comprehension. Their prejudice against business and their fear of the "alien" people pouring into American cities made it impossible for them to consider the relationships between money and art in anything but negative terms.

Such considerations are still difficult for many critics, professors, and historians. Yet, if we are asked to make any sense out of what happened in Chicago and to think at all about why it produced the greatest architecture of our time, we must accept the fact that the greatest clients of Chicago architects were businessmen and their wives. Even Henry-Russell Hitchcock, whose *Architecture: Nineteenth and Twentieth Centuries* is the standard history of modern architecture, is obviously puzzled by how Chicago with "no established traditions, no real professional leaders, and ignorance of the architectural styles, past or present" produced the great architecture of our time—an architecture which owes its existence to "enlightened commercial patrons" who "demanded and often received the best architecture of their day." He is careful to make the point that it is a mistake to disregard the architectural genius of Chicago where the "strictly *architectural*, as well as the technical and social, significance of the major commercial monuments of the nineteenth century will be evident."

The contributions of Chicago engineers to the building

art, to the creation of the city, and finally to the great Chicago Plan have often been told. Jenney's Home Insurance Building contained the first iron frame—the precursor of the steel cage. It was the first building whose walls were not load-bearing. But before the tall buildings could be built, foundations strong enough to carry their great weight in swampy soil had to be developed. Many new types of foundations were invented. Indeed, Chicago engineers were so advanced that the architects themselves were not able to keep up with them. Chicago grain elevators, which were built in the seventies on the banks of the River, used piling for foundations. Yet it was not until after 1890 that architects made common use of this type of foundation.

The new buildings of Chicago were not constructed by the city, by religious organizations, by educational institutions, or by private groups as palatial edifices. They were built by businessmen and they were built for profit. Even the Auditorium, which was the civic and cultural center of Chicago for many years, was built to make money. It was a civic center, a hotel, and an office building. It was financed like any other business venture on the expectation of profit. George H. Pullman built what he hoped would be a worker's utopia, but he made clear from the very start that, unlike the older American utopias founded by religious and co-operative groups, his utopia was strictly a business venture. The town of Pullman would prove that workers could be decently housed, fed, clothed, educated, entertained, and even worship God, at a profit to those who would build communities for them.

The women of Chicago, too, were as radical as their men —indeed, in some ways more radical. They wanted to lead public as well as private lives, and they wanted to lead simple and informal lives within the home. They wanted to be what they called "neighborly." The houses Root, and later Wright, built for them were built on "lots." These houses, unlike those in older cities, never abandoned the earlier spirit of Chicago, which, in its early days before the Fire, was known as the Garden City because of its many yards with gardens and because the number of trees which sheltered the simple one-story "cottages" built by carpenters after the elaborate Greek Revival homes of Latrobe. Chicago women did not want homes surrounded by walls, but with porches and large bay windows, open to all four sides of the yard, and close enough to the street to return greetings from neighbors. In a sense, they wanted to live in 1880 as most suburban families want to live now in the 1960's. As early as 1874 Chicagoans were boasting of their suburbs and, a few years later, of their parks along the lake front, on the West Side, and in the forest preserves.

But the achievements of Chicago businessmen, the daring and organizing ability of her builders, and the brilliance of her engineers, great though they were, do not explain the Chicago School of architecture. For the genius of architecture is formed space, and however great the community and however abundant men, money, land, and people may be, they cannot produce a great architecture without the vision and imagination of the architect. When all is said and done, Chicago did not produce great architects because it gave them the opportunity to build a city or to rebuild a city destroyed by fire. Boston and San Francisco suffered from great fires. New York, in common with many other American cities, increased rapidly in size and population. Yet Chicago, and Chicago alone, from 1875 into the 1960's, has turned to great architects for her city plan, for her buildings, for her schools, and for her homes.

This happened because of the genius of Louis H. Sullivan, who struggled through his fifty-one years of practice in Chicago (1873–1924) to create in his buildings and to communicate in his writing an aesthetic of democratic architecture. This became known as "functionalism." The spirit of functional form was the expression of the social purpose of the building in its structure. Sullivan taught that each building must be unique. He never repeated his ornament. Each building had a "spirit" which must be respected. The expression of this spirit was as much a part of its "utility" as the plumbing. For only when the building *evoked* human satisfactions determined by the form itself could it become architecture. And only when such form could be reduced to some kind of

9

principle could it become an order, and not merely a style, of architecture.

Architectural principles are reached, as Sullivan, Root, Wright, and Mies van der Rohe taught, by asking: What is the chief characteristic of the structure? To answer this for the tall building, Sullivan said that the chief characteristic of the tall office building was its loftiness. This "is the very organ-tone of its appeal. It must be in turn the dominant chord in the [architect's] expression of it, the true excitant of his imagination. It must be tall, every inch of it tall. The force and power of altitude must be in it, the glory and pride of exaltation must be in it. It must be every inch a proud and soaring thing, rising in sheer exaltation that from bottom to top it is a unit without a single dissenting line. . . ."

The deeper principle underlying the character of the soaring tower is that the outward expression, structure, "design or whatever we may choose [to call it], of the tall office building should in the very nature of things follow the functions of the building. . . ." Architectural art has failed thus far, Sullivan taught, because it has not yet found a way to become truly plastic: "It does not yield to the poet's touch." It is the only art "for which the multitudinous rhythms of outward nature, the manifold fluctuations of man's inner being have no significance, no place." Greek architecture, great as it was, lacked rhythm because it was not related to nature, and because the great art of music had not been born. While possessing serenity, "it lacked the divinely human element of mobility." Gothic architecture, "with sombre ecstatic eye," evolved a copious and rich variety of expression, but it "lacked the unitary comprehension, the absolute consciousness and mastery of pure form that can come alone of unclouded and serene contemplation, of perfect repose and peace of mind."

Thus, while the Greek knew the "statics, the Goth the dynamics," of architecture, neither of them suspected the mobile equilibrium of it, because neither of them "divined the movement and stability of nature."

Failing in this, both have fallen short, "and must pass away when the true, the *Poetic Architecture* shall arise—

that architecture which shall speak with clearness, with eloquence, and with warmth, of the fullness, the completeness of man's intercourse with nature and with his fellow men." The search for a new kind of movement in architecture, which Sullivan called "mobile equilibrium," is the clue to the aesthetics of the Chicago School of the past, as it is to Mies van der Rohe's work in the present.

When we look at Chicago's towers, we sense at once the tension between horizontal and vertical thrust. The resolution of this tension creates a "mobile equilibrium." As our eye travels up the massive flanks of the Monadnock, along the glass bays of the Reliance, the steel piers of 860–80 Lake Shore Drive, or the Inland Steel Company Building, we experience at once the soaring quality of the great tower. We are freed from earth and carried up into the sky. We are no longer earthbound: a new kind of power fills our being as a sense of movement—movement into the sky—sweeps over us. But the eye also rests on horizontal planes whose intersection with the vertical thrust arrests the eyes long enough to make our upward flight a rhythmic progression, not a headlong rush into space. The horizontal plane acts like a musical phrase.

Sometimes the spirit of form is horizontal; at other times it is vertical. Carson Pirie Scott, the Robie House, the Illinois Institute of Technology Campus, accentuate horizontal planes. For Sullivan, Wright, and Jens Jensen, the great landscape architect, the horizontal line was the prairie line, the great rolling prairie of the Middle West which moved our artists so deeply. Wright, speaking for every middle western artist, said: "I loved the prairie by instinct as, itself, a great simplicity; the trees, the flowers, and sky were thrilling by contrast . . . the plain . . . serene beneath a wonderful sweep of sky." The horizontal plane becomes one of movement, flow, and continuity. And it is the human plane, the plane along which man walks with other men. The vertical thrust gives us a sense of power, but the horizontal brings us serenity and peace.

And this, in the last analysis, is the power of these great Chicago buildings. They are a humane expression of a new

11

way of life—the modern urban community based on money and technology. They are humane because the architects of the Chicago School, from the first generation of the seventies and eighties to the third generation of the sixties in our century, have followed the teachings of their master, Sullivan. "With me," he said, "architecture is not an art, but a religion, and that religion but a part of democracy." In this spirit our best buildings and communities have been—and will be—designed. The love of the common man has been the glory of Chicago. The belief that only when he is decently housed can democracy survive has been the moral glory of our architecture. The conviction that he must be beautifully housed and sheltered has become the aesthetic credo of modern architecture. Who is to do this—the state, the businessman, or the powerful institutions of the democratic community itself—is by no means certain. But that it *must* be done is certain. For democracy cannot exist without good architecture, and good architecture in turn can be created only among men who walk the earth in freedom and dignity.

The Chicago School: ... and Practice

BY CARL W. CONDIT

In the chaos of architectural styles that prevails today, Chicago has reasserted its great building tradition in a body of work that may be traced directly back to the days when the city launched the modern movement in architecture and structural techniques. The motives behind this contemporary resurgence include negative as well as positive aspects. One is a reaction against the slick and faceless curtain wall of most commercial building, that shallow and often gaudy wrapping that makes us wonder whether architecture is no more than a variation on the art of packaging. On the positive side, the architects are seeking again to exploit the potentially dynamic quality of the structural frame of steel and concrete, and to explore the possibilities of new variations on older framing techniques. Whatever the motive, it is clear that the current work represents a deliberate return to the basic principle of the Chicago School: an aesthetic statement, developed through structure, of the necessary physical character of the building.

The original Chicago School of architecture, from its inception to its last days, flourished over the half-century that extended from 1875 to 1925. By 1910 the movement had produced an original, indigenous, and organic architecture for every kind of building—office skyscrapers, hotels and apartments, warehouses and factories, residences, schools, and churches. In the extraordinary decades of the eighties and nineties, the architects and engineers of Chicago developed the structural system of the contemporary multistory building and most of the essential forms of modern architecture. "Here is where it all began," as the editors of *Architectural Forum* recently wrote.

From the beginning this movement divided into two major streams whose leading figures were William Le Baron Jenney and Louis H. Sullivan. Jenney was a strict utilitarian, an empiricist who sought the most economical forms of building to satisfy the functional requirements. His aims were maximum efficiency and economy of construction, open interior space, and the maximum admission of natural light. The external form that grew out of this program is distinguished mainly by the articulated or cellular wall of "Chicago windows," a basic rectangular pattern corresponding in its geometry to the underlying frame of iron or steel and surmounting an open base of glass like a continuous transparent screen. Sullivan, on the other hand, was a self-conscious romantic who treated a building as a plastic object molded to give expression to the strong feeling that the new technology aroused in him.

In spite of Jenney's narrow approach, his influence led to a great diversity of forms derived organically from the underlying skeletal structure. It is best revealed by the work of Holabird and Roche, the most prolific of the Chicago architects during the heroic age. Sullivan's work tended to be subjective, somewhat at odds with the impersonal commercial spirit, and his legacy was passed on chiefly to Frank Lloyd Wright, his greatest and most famous protégé.

If we look carefully at a few of the more famous buildings of the original Chicago School, we can readily see in them the spiritual ancestry of the best contemporary designs. The articulated wall of rectangular cells became the primary visual feature of these first representatives of a new architectural style. Even the exposed steelwork of such recent buildings as the Continental Center and the Civic Center was anticipated long ago in the iron spandrel plates in the facade of the old Brunswick (originally Studebaker) Building, designed by Solon S. Beman and erected at 629 South Wabash Avenue in 1895. The same feature appears in the spandrel plates at the first story of Jenney's Sears Roebuck Store, at

State and Van Buren streets, and in his Manhattan Building, at 431 South Dearborn Street, both completed by 1891.

Sullivan's Carson Pirie Scott Store, the masterpiece of the Chicago School and America's greatest work of commercial architecture, represents a formal elaboration of the principle of structural form. Here the neutral cage of iron and steel is transformed into fine architecture through Sullivan's unerring sense of proportion, his ornamental skill, and his exact calculation of the depth of the window reveals to give maximum power to the elevation.

The horizontal elongation of wide-bayed framing appears most strikingly in the huge concrete warehouse of Montgomery Ward and Company, designed by Schmidt, Garden and Martin. The architects of this building deliberately intensified the natural horizontality of the long bands of concrete girders. The same motif distinguishes Wright's Robie House, although here it is developed into a complex pattern of intersecting planes. The Carson Store was completed in 1906, the warehouse in 1908. Fifty years later these features of what was once known as the "Chicago style" were again becoming prominent in the city's buildings.

The opening of the masonry bearing wall in a way that anticipates the contemporary load-bearing truss of concrete is most apparent in Burnham and Root's classic Monadnock Building (1889–91), an austere geometric refinement of the rich dress of their earlier Rookery (1885–86). The projecting bay of the Monadnock was first adapted to the multistory commercial block by Holabird and Roche, but it was given its purest expression by Clinton J. Warren in the Congress Hotel. (Warren designed the original north block, completed in 1893, but Holabird and Roche followed his program in the later south wing, opened, as it now is, in 1907.) The Congress, recently renovated, remains one of the finest works of hotel design in the United States.

Europe could offer no parallel to the Chicago movement at its height. When the leading pioneers—Le Corbusier, Gropius, Mies van der Rohe—began to win attention, even their best designs seemed coldly abstract beside the great

15

richness and variety of the Chicago work. In one of the ironies of our cultural history, however, when modern architecture revived in the United States, it did so under the impetus of European importations. It was an old story—the distrust of native achievements, the belief that Europe must always be the fountainhead of new artistic and intellectual creations. The early work of the European pioneers revealed a sure mastery of the new structural techniques and their formal possibilities, but it was a prime misfortune that the so-called International Style should have swept everything else before it.

This state of affairs continued for nearly two decades, from 1930 to 1950, when the modern movement in the United States was rapidly winning its triumph over the eclecticism of the immediate past. The revolutionary structural inventions of our century, especially reinforced concrete shells, plates, and prestressed members, like the new architectural forms, were all of European origin. With the enormous volume of building that came after World War II, the new inventions spread into such a variety of forms that the idea of a consistent style became an anachronism. Indeed, the long-debated questions—what have we accomplished and where are we going?—are more controversial than ever.

The new Chicago School was established primarily by Mies van der Rohe, who has enjoyed an unbroken series of major commissions in the building boom that followed the war. The Promontory Apartments on South Lake Shore Drive near 56th Street (1948–49) is the first of Mies's fourteen apartment towers that stand singly or in groups along the lakeshore or at the west edge of Lincoln Park. Promontory is unique among these internationally celebrated buildings and belongs exactly to the idiom of the Chicago School. It is the first one in which the naked concrete frame provides the dominant features of the elevation. The outermost columns and girders stand out strong and clear, each rectangular bay enframing a sweep of glass surmounting the narrow spandrel of brick.

Promontory was immediately influential in apartment design. Pace Associates carried the principle to its logical ulti-

16

mate in the apartment building at the southeast corner of Sheridan Road and Oakdale Avenue (1951–52), where the street and rear elevations are reduced to the exposed concrete frame alone, the entire bay being filled with glass. Since then, the articulated wall of exposed framing members, brick spandrels, and glass has appeared in many large apartment projects, most notably the quarter-circular building at 1150 North Lake Shore Drive, designed by Hausner and Macsai, and the Imperial Towers and Sandburg Village of Solomon and Cordwell.

Meanwhile, Mies had turned to steel construction and offered a strikingly different structural form in Crown Hall, built in 1955–56 on the campus of the Illinois Institute of Technology. The building is a single enclosure of glass supported by four welded rigid frames prominently displayed outside the building envelope. The result is a technical and aesthetic masterpiece of pure geometric form.

But Mies preferred the delicate vertical tracery of the later apartments and IIT buildings. The Chicago tradition in its original character passed to the hands of the enormously prolific firm of Skidmore, Owings and Merrill. Their Inland Steel Building, at Monroe and Dearborn streets (1955–57), is a remarkable *tour de force* in the expression of welded steel framing. The 19-story glass prism contains no interior columns, the primary bearing elements being seven pairs of columns located outside the planes of the long elevations. The floors are carried on transverse girders of 58-foot clear span, a characteristic which makes the Inland Steel Building the first of the wide-bayed structures that are now the hallmark of Chicago building. A novel feature in the planning of the Inland is the separation of elevators and utilities into a tower set wholly apart from the rental area of the main block. The entire building volume is thus divided into the "served" and "servant" areas that Louis I. Kahn later made famous in the brick and concrete structure of the Richards Medical Research Laboratory at the University of Pennsylvania.

The Skidmore firm dropped the Miesian tracery of the Inland Steel in favor of unadorned engineering in the Hartford Insurance Building, built in 1960–61 at Wacker Drive and Monroe Streets. If the Inland is the celebration of technique, the Hartford is technique itself. All one sees here are the columns and floor edges of the flat-slab framing, a system of reinforced concrete construction without beams and girders. The building represents the ultimate in purification of the Chicago style, sharpened and intensified by the functional device of setting the window planes well back from the outer edges of the framing members.

The enthusiasm for wide-bayed steel framing gathered momentum. The traditional skeleton was greatly elongated on horizontal planes in the Continental Center, designed by C. F. Murphy Associates and built in 1961–62 at Wabash Avenue and Jackson Boulevard. Another building with a column-free interior, it is square in plan, the 42-foot bays disposed around three sides of a central court enclosing elevators and utilities. The peculiar combination of force and dignity in the elevations of the Continental Center arises from a strictly empirical approach. The depth of girder required by the wide bay immediately raises the question: How can one justify this costly sacrifice of vertical space? It is a case of structure scientifically designed for economy and utility: the girders are deep enough to allow ducts and conduits to pass through them; the large bays reduce the number of columns and hence the expensive foundation and caisson work of the Chicago region; and the deep girders, rigidly fixed to the columns, provide the necessary stability against wind without any other bracing elements.

Certain features of the Continental design are particularly significant for the new aesthetic currents. The naked steelwork of the street elevations is painted a flat black, the perfect antithesis to the glittering package of the advertisers and its equivalent in most contemporary architecture. The floors and partitions of the lobby are unpolished granite, hard, rough-textured, and durable, suggesting a deliberate choice of surface harshness.

C. F. Murphy Associates, chief architects, with Skidmore, Owings and Merrill, and Loebl, Schlossman and Bennett as

18

associated architects, carried the principle of wide-bayed framing to a climax in their staggering design for Chicago's new Civic Center, under construction since 1963 on the block bounded by Dearborn, Washington, Clark, and Randolph streets. The 648-foot tower—the highest in Chicago at the time of its completion—will be carried on 16 massive primary columns set for a maximum span of 87 feet. This unprecedented spacing requires an underfloor system of beams in the form of trusses with a uniform depth of 5 feet 6 inches. The depth of the floor trusses was calculated for the load on the maximum span but held uniform for shorter spans again to allow the passage of ducts and conduits through the floor framing. The huge members of the steel skeleton will be left unpainted on the exterior, the special metal allowed to oxidize to a natural patina of dark red-brown. There is something almost brutal in this assertion of technical virtuosity. For sheer articulated power the Civic Center stands by itself among American skyscrapers, a statement of physical laws on a grand scale.

Across the street from the plaza of the Center stands the Brunswick Building, constructed at the same time as its neighbor to the north. Another triumph of SOM engineering, the Brunswick was the largest building at the time of its construction with external walls of rigid-frame concrete trusses (also known as load-bearing screen walls and window truss walls). A wall of this kind is the most recent structural innovation in American building and springs from a long and complex history. The actual truss form was invented in 1896 by the Belgian engineer M. A. Vierendeel originally for steel-bridge construction. It was adapted to concrete framing and first used for the entire area of building walls in the University Apartments, designed by I. M. Pei and Loewenburg and Loewenburg and built in 1959–61 at University Avenue and 55th Street near the University of Chicago. The application of the Vierendeel truss to building walls may be thought of as a combination of the traditional masonry-bearing wall and the articulated or cellular curtain of the Chicago School. The aesthetic virtue of the load-bearing screen is that it brings back to the wall the texture, depth, and mass that we miss in the monotonous and brittle curtain of glass and enameled steel. Again, the interior of the Brunswick is column-free, and the elevator bays are enclosed in solid concrete walls which provide resistance to wind loads. The wall loads of the building are carried to the columns of the base by a peripheral girder 24 feet 5½ inches deep, occupying the combined height of the second and third stories.

In the conventional form of column-and-beam framing, Skidmore, Owings and Merrill used another extreme bay span in the United Air Lines building in Elk Grove. The 66-foot bays were made possible by the use of prestressed girders, one of the major building inventions of the twentieth century. The long bays and the two-story height give the UAL buildings an exaggerated horizontality, nicely appropriate to their open, level prairie setting.

Outside the ruling mode of structural expression there are other rediscoveries of the earlier Chicago work. The most welcome is the revival of the projecting bay, or oriel, that chiefly marked the hotels and apartments of the Chicago School. Two good examples stand among the imaginative designs of Harry Weese. The first is the apartment at 227 East Walton Street, opened in 1955, exactly planned for both light and privacy on a narrow lot and narrower street. More prominent because of its open site is Stanley R. Pierce Hall, completed in 1960 as a dormitory for the University of Chicago. The oriel windows of this building were designed primarily to break up the flat curtain of brick and glass into a multiplicity of light-reflecting planes. The same device is used on a larger scale but less successfully in the long elevation of the Michigan Terrace Apartments, opened in 1963 at Michigan and Grand avenues. Here the projections are set so close together that each one in effect blocks out those on either side of it.

The towers of Bertrand Goldberg's Marina City, erected in 1960–64, constitute another stunning exhibition of structural virtuosity, but their background follows a different historical cycle. The cylindrical cores that share the vertical loads with the peripheral columns and provide resistance to the lateral forces of the wind go back to the principle of core-and-cantilever construction, which was first proposed by Mies van der Rohe in 1919 for a Berlin skyscraper that was never built, nor has it been used for any of his Chicago buildings. The system was first embodied in the Research Tower of S. C. Johnson and Company at Racine, Wisconsin (1947–50), designed by the former Chicagoan, Frank Lloyd Wright. Thus, partly by historical coincidence, this form also seems appropriate to the Chicago tradition.

To elucidate the full meaning of the new Chicago work for the general development of modern architecture would require an extensive historical and aesthetic analysis. It is possible, however, to get at the essence of it in a few generalizations. The great historical styles of architecture, as these appear in monumental works such as ecclesiastical and civic buildings, may be regarded in essence as the symbolic images of some kind of cosmos—divine, natural, or political, depending on the views of the age. In the absence of any public agreement on the nature of an encompassing order, modern architecture has repeated the history of the Chicago School in continuing its two basic approaches to formal design. One seeks a personal statement that increasingly moves toward plastic self-expression. This stream was long dominated by Frank Lloyd Wright, while after his death it came to be associated mainly with the pictorial formalism of architects such as Louis I. Kahn and Paul Rudolph. The other approach tries to find a more public and objective image, and by necessity turns to the laws of physical science as they are embodied in scientific structural design.

The second category is easily the larger of the two. Its pervasiveness is clearly attested by the influence of engineers like Pier Luigi Nervi and by the steady outpouring of books composed around the theme that structure and form are identical. But this form arises from the exigencies of utilitarianism and technical requirements and is thus essentially empirical. The new Chicago movement belongs in good part to the technological approach. Technical details are developed as symbols for the mathematical-scientific concepts underlying the structure. The emotional impact of such building arises mainly from the evocation of kinesthetic images; the experience it offers is a formal intensification of that provided by great engineering works such as bridges, dams, and other pure structural revelations.

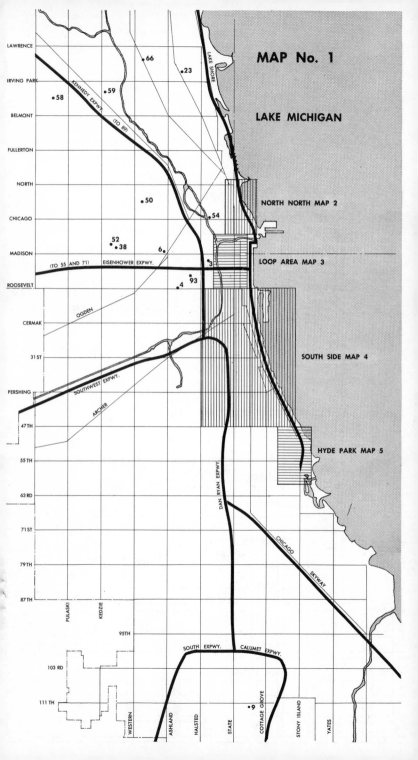

MAP No. 1

LAKE MICHIGAN

NORTH NORTH MAP 2

LOOP AREA MAP 3

SOUTH SIDE MAP 4

HYDE PARK MAP 5

LAWRENCE

IRVING PARK

BELMONT

FULLERTON

NORTH

CHICAGO

MADISON

ROOSEVELT

CERMAK

31 ST

PERSHING

47TH

55TH

63 RD

71ST

79TH

87TH

95TH

103 RD

111 TH

LAKE SHORE

KENNEDY EXPWY. (TO 89)

(TO 55 AND 71) EISENHOWER EXPWY.

OGDEN

SOUTHWEST EXPWY.

ARCHER

DAN RYAN EXPWY

CHICAGO SKYWAY

SOUTH EXPWY. CALUMET EXPWY.

PULASKI

KEDZIE

WESTERN

ASHLAND

HALSTED

STATE

COTTAGE GROVE

STONY ISLAND

YATES

•66

•23

•59

•58

•50

•54

•52
•38

6•

•3

•4 •93

•9

MAP No. 2

LINCOLN PARK

LAKE MICHIGAN

NORTH

• 77

49 •

BURTON

SCHILLER

• 29

GOETHE

ASTOR

LAKE SHORE

DIVISION

ELM

MAPLE

CEDAR

30 •

BELLEVUE

OAK

31 •

WALTON

• 70

DELAWARE

62 •

CHESTNUT

75 •

PEARSON

5 •

CHICAGO

SUPERIOR

HURON

11 •

ERIE

ONTARIO

WELLS

LA SALLE

CLARK

DEARBORN

OHIO

STATE

WABASH

RUSH

MICHIGAN

ST. CLAIR

FAIRBANKS

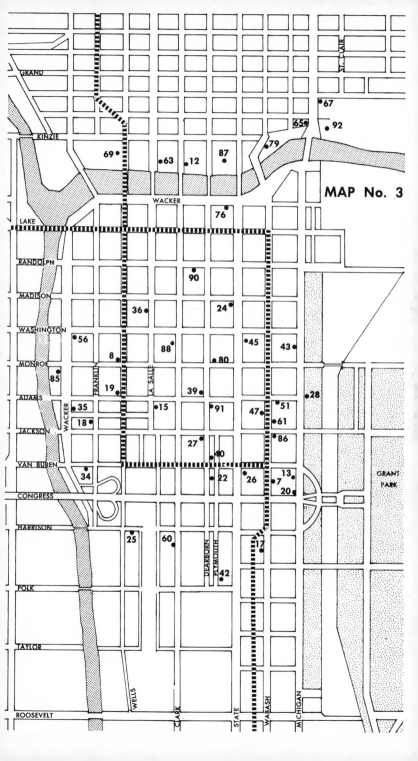

MAP No. 3

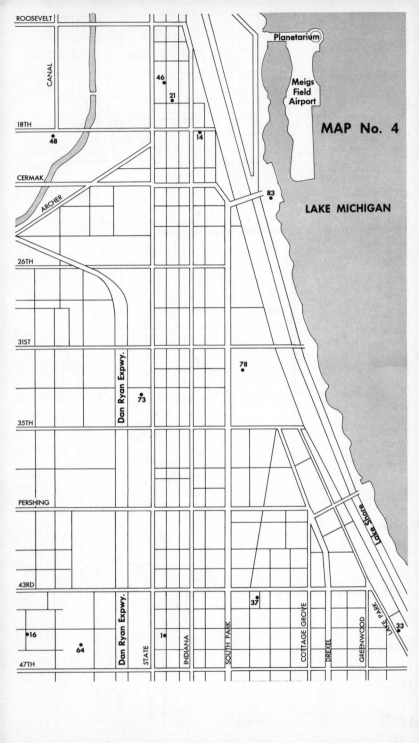

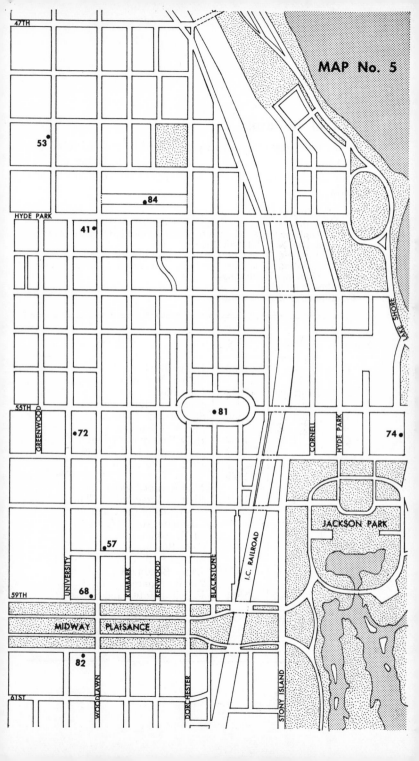

MAP No. 5

47TH

53

84

HYDE PARK

41

55TH

GREENWOOD

72

81

CORNELL

HYDE PARK

74

LAKE SHORE

JACKSON PARK

57

UNIVERSITY

KIMBARK

KENWOOD

BLACKSTONE

I.C. RAILROAD

59TH

68

MIDWAY PLAISANCE

82

WOODLAWN

DORCHESTER

STONY ISLAND

61ST

List of Buildings

The following categories were selected by the Commission on Chicago Architectural Landmarks for the listing of the buildings included in this volume (see column six in the table below):

I. Buildings of historic importance
    A. Buildings of symbolic or sentimental importance
    B. Buildings in which events of importance have taken place
II. Buildings of architectural merit
    A. Buildings of architectural merit, in historic styles
    B. Buildings of architectural merit, in style of Chicago School (Landmark Buildings)
III. Recent buildings
IV. Buildings of general interest

Building Number	Map	Date	Building
1	4	1836	Henry B. Clarke House 4526 S. Wabash
2	Destroyed	1852	Lind Block Wacker at Randolph
3	1	1856	St. Patrick's Church 718 W. Adams
4	1	1860 1869	Holy Family Church and St. Ignatius High School 1072 W. Roosevelt
5	2	1869	Water Tower Michigan at Chicago
6	1	1871	First Congregational Church (originally the Union Park Congregational Church) 44 N. Ashland
7	3	1875	Giles Building 423–29 S. Wabash
8	3	1879	Leiter Building I 208 W. Monroe
9	1	1881	Florence Hotel (and Square) 11111 S. Forestville
10	Destroyed	1882	Hammond Library Union Theological College Ashland at Warren

It was the decision of the committee that attribution should be made as of the date of the initiation of the project.

NOTE.—In the photographic guide, beginning on page 1, the Landmark Buildings selected by the Commission as masterworks of the Chicago School are designated by a capital **L.**

Architect	Category	Building Number
Unknown	I–A	1
Unknown	I–A	2
Unknown	II–A	3
John M. van Osdel(?) Unknown	I–A	4
W. W. Boyington	II–A	5
Gordon P. Randall	I–A	6
Otis L. Wheelock	II–A	7
William L. Jenney	Landmark	8
S. S. Beman	II–A	9
Adler and Sullivan	I–A	10

Building Number	Map	Date	Building
11	2	1883	Nickerson Residence 40 E. Erie

12	3	1883	Central Cold Storage Warehouse
			   (originally the Hiram Sibley
			   Warehouse)
			315–31 N. Clark

13	3	1884	Fine Arts Building
			   (originally the Studebaker
			   Building)
			410 S. Michigan

14	4	1886	Glessner House 1800 S. Prairie
15	3	1886	Rookery Building 209 S. LaSalle
16	4	1887	St. Gabriel's Church 4501 S. Lowe
17	3	1887	Wirt Dexter Building 630 S. Wabash

18	3	1887	Willoughby Building
			   (now the 234 S. Franklin
			   Building)

19	3	1888	200 W. Adams Building
20	3	1889	Auditorium Building Michigan at Congress

21	4	1890	First Infantry Armory
			   (later the 131st Infantry
			   Armory)
			Michigan at 16th

22	3	1890	Manhattan Building 431 S. Dearborn
23	1	1890	Getty Tomb Graceland Cemetery 4001 N. Clark
24	3	1895	Reliance Building 32 N. State

25	3	1890	Grand Central Station
			   (originally Wisconsin Central
			   Station)
			Wells at Harrison

26	3	1891	Sears, Roebuck and Co. (originally Leiter Building II) Van Buren at State
27	3	1891	Monadnock Building 53 W. Jackson
28	3	1892	The Art Institute Michigan at Adams

Architect	Category	Building Number
Burling and Whitehouse	II–A	11
George H. Edbrooke	II–A	12
S. S. Beman	IV	13
Henry H. Richardson	Landmark	14
Burnham and Root	Landmark	15
Burnham and Root	II–B	16
Adler and Sullivan	Landmark	17
Leroy S. Buffington(?)	II–B	18
Burling and Whitehouse	II–B	19
Adler and Sullivan	Landmark	20
Burnham and Root	I–B	21
William L. Jenney	II–B	22
Louis H. Sullivan	Landmark	23
D. H. Burnham and Co.	Landmark	24
S. S. Beman	II–A	25
Jenney and Mundie	II–B	26
Burnham and Root	Landmark	27
Shepley, Rutan and Coolidge	IV	28

Building Number	Map	Date	Building
29	2	1892	Charnley House 1365 N. Astor
30	2	1892	Fortnightly Club (originally the Lathrop House) 120 E. Bellevue
31	2	1892	Newberry Library 60 W. Walton
32	Destroyed	1892	Garrick Building (originally the Schiller Building) 64 W. Randolph
33	4	1892	Sullivan House 4575 S. Lake Park
34	3	1893	Meyer Building 307 W. Van Buren

35	3	1892	Yondorf Building
			    (now the 225–29 S. Wacker
			    Building)

36	3	1894	The Old Chicago Stock Exchange 30 N. LaSalle
37	4	1895	Francis Apartments 4304 S. Forestville
38	1	1895	Francisco Terrace Apartments 253–57 N. Francisco
39	3	1895	Marquette Building 140 S. Dearborn
40	3	1896	Fisher Building 343 S. Dearborn
41	5	1897	Heller House 5132 S. Woodlawn

42	3	1897	731 S. Plymouth Building
			    (originally the Lakeside Press
			    Building)

43	3	1898	Gage Building 18 S. Michigan
44	Destroyed	1899	Cable Building 57 E. Jackson

45	3	1899,
		1903–4
			Carson Pirie Scott Store
			    (originally the Schlesinger and
			    Mayer Store)
			State at Madison

46	4	1900	The Coliseum 1513 S. Wabash
47	3	1900	Crown Building (originally the McClurg Building) 218 S. Wabash

Architect	Category	Building Number
Adler and Sullivan (Design: Frank Lloyd Wright)	Landmark	29
McKim, Mead and White	II–A	30
Henry I. Cobb	IV	31
Adler and Sullivan	Landmark	32
Adler and Sullivan	Landmark	33
Adler and Sullivan	Landmark	34
Unknown	II–B	35
Adler and Sullivan	Landmark	36
Frank Lloyd Wright	Landmark	37
Frank Lloyd Wright	II–B	38
Holabird and Roche	II–B	39
D. H. Burnham and Co.	Landmark	40
Frank Lloyd Wright	Landmark	41
Howard V. Shaw	II–B	42
Holabird and Roche (Facade: Louis H. Sullivan)	Landmark	43
Holabird and Roche	Landmark	44
Louis H. Sullivan	Landmark	45
Frost and Granger	I–B	46
Holabird and Roche	Landmark	47

Building Number	Map	Date	Building
48	4	1902	Schoenhofen Brewery Co. (now Morningstar-Paisley Co.) 18th at Canalport
49	2	1902	Madlener House (now the Graham Foundation) 4 W. Burton
50	1	1903	Holy Trinity Russian Orthodox Cathedral 1121 N. Leavitt
51	3	1904	Chapin and Gore Building (now the 63 E. Adams Building)
52	1	1905	E-Z Polish Building (now Universal Foods Corp.) 3005 W. Carroll
53	5	1906	Magerstadt House 4930 S. Greenwood
54	1	1907	Montgomery Ward and Co. Warehouse 618 W. Chicago
55	1	1908	Our Lady of Lebanon Church (originally the First Congregational Church of Austin) Waller and Midway Park
56	3	1908	Liberty Mutual Insurance Building (originally the Hunter Building) 337 W. Madison
57	5	1909	Robie House 5757 S. Woodlawn
58	1	1909	Carl Schurz High School Milwaukee at Addison
59	1	1910	Grover Cleveland Elementary School 3850 N. Albany
60	3	1911	Dwight Building 626 S. Clark
61	3	1912	Edison Shop (now Hung Fa Village Restaurant) 229 S. Wabash
62	2	1912	Fourth Presbyterian Church and Parish House 126 E. Chestnut
63	3	1913	City of Chicago Central Office Building (originally Reid, Murdoch and Co.) 325 N. LaSalle

Architect	Category	Building Number
Richard E. Schmidt (Design: Hugh Garden)	Landmark	48
Richard E. Schmidt	Landmark	49
Louis H. Sullivan	II–A	50
Richard E. Schmidt	Landmark	51
Frank Lloyd Wright	Landmark	52
George W. Maher	Landmark	53
Schmidt, Garden and Martin	II–B	54
Guenzel and Drummond	Landmark	55
Christian A. Eckstrom	Landmark	56
Frank Lloyd Wright	Landmark	57
Dwight H. Perkins	Landmark	58
Dwight H. Perkins	Landmark	59
Schmidt, Garden and Martin	Landmark	60
Purcell, Feick and Elmslie	Landmark	61
R. A. Cram and H. V. Shaw	II–A	62
George C. Nimmons	Landmark	63

Building Number	Map	Date	Building
64	4	1915	Park Buildings, Fuller Park 45th at Princeton
65	3	1921, 1924	Wrigley Building N. Michigan at the River
66	1	1922	Krause Music Store (now Arnzen-Coleman Co.) 4611 N. Lincoln
67	3	1922	Tribune Tower N. Michigan at the River
68	5	1928	Rockefeller Memorial Chapel 59th at Woodlawn
69	3	1929–30	Merchandise Mart North Bank
70	2	1929–30	Palmolive Building 919 N. Michigan
71	1	1937	Third Unitarian Church 301 N. Mayfield
72	5	1937	University Building 5551 S. University
73	4	1942–58	Illinois Institute of Technology Campus 32d at State
74	5	1949	Promontory Apartments 5530 S. Shore
75	2	1952	860–80 Lake Shore Drive Apartments
76	3	1955	City Parking Facility ("Bird Cage") 11 W. Wacker
77	2	1956	Chess Pavilion Lincoln Park
78	4	1956–60	Lake Meadows 31st to 35th and South Park
79	3	1957	Sun-Times Building N. Wabash at the River
80	3	1957	Inland Steel Building 30 W. Monroe
81	5	1959	Hyde Park Redevelopment
82	5	1960	Law School, University of Chicago 1121 E. 60th

Architect	Category	Building Number
Edward H. Bennett	II–B	64
Graham, Anderson, Probst and White	IV	65
Louis H. Sullivan William C. Presto	Landmark	66
Hood and Howells	IV	67
Bertram W. Goodhue	II–A	68
Graham, Anderson, Probst and White	IV	69
Holabird and Root	IV	70
Paul Schweiker, Inc.	Landmark	71
F. Fred Keck and William Keck	Landmark	72
Mies van der Rohe Friedman, Alschuler and Sincere Holabird and Root Pace Associates	Landmark	73
Mies van der Rohe Pace Associates Holsman, Holsman and Taylor	II–B	74
Mies van der Rohe Pace Associates Holsman, Holsman, Klekamp and Taylor	Landmark	75
Shaw, Metz and Dolio	III	76
Morris Webster	III	77
Skidmore, Owings and Merrill	II-B	78
Naess and Murphy	IV	79
Skidmore, Owings and Merrill	Landmark	80
I. M. Pei and Harry Weese	IV	81
Eero Saarinen	III	82

Building Number	Map	Date	Building
83	4	1960	McCormick Place 23d at Lake Front
84	5	1961	Atrium Houses 1370 E. Madison Park
85	3	1961	Hartford Insurance Building 100 S. Wacker
86	3	1962	Continental Insurance Building 55 E. Jackson
87	3	1964	Marina City 300 N. State
88	3	1963	Loop Synagogue 16 S. Clark
89	1	1963	Chicago O'Hare International Airport Northwest City Limits
90	3	1964–65	Chicago Civic Center Randolph, Washington, Dearborn, and Clark
91	3	In construction	Chicago Federal Center Dearborn from Adams to Jackson
92	3	1965	Equitable Building Michigan at the River
93	1	1965–67	University of Illinois Chicago Campus Harrison at Halsted

Architect	Category	Building Number
Shaw, Metz and Associates	IV	83
Y. C. Wong	III	84
Skidmore, Owings and Merrill	III	85
C. F. Murphy Associates	III	86
Bertrand Goldberg Associates	IV	87
Loebel, Schlossman and Bennett	III	88
Naess and Murphy	IV	89
C. F. Murphy Associates Skidmore, Owings and Merrill Loebl, Schlossman and Bennett	IV	90
Mies van der Rohe Schmidt, Garden and Erickson C. F. Murphy Associates A. Epstein and Sons, Inc.	IV	91
Skidmore, Owings and Merrill Alfred Shaw, Associated	IV	92
Skidmore, Owings and Merrill C. F. Murphy Associates A. Epstein and Sons, Inc.	IV	93

1. Henry B. Clarke House. 1836. I-A
Architect unknown.
4526 South Wabash (45 E). Map 4.

Sometimes known as the Widow Clarke House, this is the oldest building still standing in Chicago, although it was moved from its original site near 16th Street and Michigan. Its portico, or porch, has been removed, as well as the original tall window shutters. But the proportions, the placing of the windows, and even the tower-like cupola on top, remain. The influence of classical models is seen in the low-pitched gable on the front, as well as in the simple moldings. The spaciousness of the first elegant homes of the city is suggested by the triple-sashed windows, which tell of the high-ceilinged rooms within.

2. Lind Block. 1852.
   Architect unknown.
   North Wacker (360 W) and West Randolph (150 N).
   Destroyed, 1963.

A structure often called a "block" in the early days, this was
one of the city's earliest business buildings. Very simple in
form, it had only a few classical details, intended to make it
"architecture." The narrow arched windows had the small
scale and provincial charm also seen in those of the cupola
of the Clarke House (No. 1).

3. St. Patrick's Church. 1854. II-A
Architect unknown.
718 West Adams (200 S). Map 1.

An early church in the Romanesque style (often called Norman in the 1850's), exemplified by round arches, narrow windows, and broad, massive walls. Typical of this style also are the arched "corbel-tables" (thickened horizontal strips of wall, carried on masonry projections called "corbels," here connected by small arches against the wall). The small octagonal towers are not ineffective, given the small scale of all the elements—for instance, the narrow arched windows (compare Nos. 1 and 2). Originally the center of the facade ended in a gable at the top, and there were no belfry stories or spires on the towers (although they doubtless were intended from the beginning).

4. Holy Family Church. 1860. I-A
Architect: John M. van Osdel?
St. Ignatius High School (College). 1869.
Architect unknown.
1076 and 1072 West Roosevelt (1200 S). Map 1.

A great barnlike building of brick, this church follows the Gothic style, as seen in the pointed arches found not only over the large openings but also as small components of the "corbel-tables" (compare No. 3). Alternation of windows and buttresses in the walls of the side aisles results in a simple rhythm of some interest; but throughout the building one is struck most by a self-conscious and artificial use of Gothic details, as in the combination of a pointed arch and a gable in relief over it, found both on the exterior and in the interior. The facade is of painted-over brick; and the interior piers are also of brick but covered with stucco in imitation of stone. The smaller tower is of stone and the larger one of sheet metal.

Various parts of the present church were built at different dates, and several architects were involved, of whom van Osdel was one. He apparently designed, or carried out from some other architect's design, the original facade and the main body of the church, both finished in 1860; and presumably he also executed the transepts, finished in 1862. In 1866 the facade was torn down and rebuilt, wider and some distance south of its original location, in order to enlarge the church in that direction, the central part being rebuilt exactly as before. The larger tower (designed by Judas Huber) was built in 1874. The adjacent high school (college) is considerably more attractive than the church because of its greater simplicity and directness, but I do not know of any evidence to show who its architect was.

5. Water Tower. 1869.   II-A
Architect: W. W. Boyington.
North Michigan (100 E) at Chicago (800 N). Map 2.

An imitation of Gothic architecture so naïve that it seems
original at points, as in the cut-stone "battlements" at the
top of the lower wall sections. Oscar Wilde, on his visit to
Chicago in 1882, called it "a castellated monstrosity with
pepper boxes stuck all over it," although he praised the
pumping machinery as "simple, grand and natural." Today
it has the character of a museum piece and is kept by Chicago on its most prominent avenue in conscious commemo-
ration of the past, particularly of the fact that, alone among
the buildings in the area, it survived the Great Fire of 1871.

6. First Congregational Church. 1871. I-A

(Originally the Union Park Congregational Church.)
Architect: Gordon P. Randall.
44 North Ashland (1600 W). Map 1.

This building is typical of a number of churches, built shortly
before and after the Great Fire, which followed the Gothic
style but in a free, sometimes inventive, manner. They
were often built of the local limestone called Joliet stone or
Lemont limestone (or even "Athens marble") seen in this
church. A large plaque in the north wall of the tower gives
the original name and dates the laying of the cornerstone as
1869. The interior is noteworthy. The shallow transepts hardly show, except in the ceiling, so that the interior becomes
a single centralized space, dominated by a dramatic balcony.
This begins as a continuation of the choir space behind the
pulpit, then sweeps in a great circle around the auditorium,
rising and becoming rapidly wider toward the back. The
result is an impressive adaptation to congregational use, the
minister being placed as it were in the midst of the congre-
gation. (The structure was strengthened in 1927, but apparently without changing the architectural forms.)

7. Giles Building. 1875.
(Now the 423–29 South Wabash Building.)
Architect: Otis L. Wheelock.
423–29 South Wabash (45 E). Map 3.

Built just after the Fire, this is the most nearly intact of the office buildings that followed French fashion and were said to be in the "Mansard" style. The top story of the Giles still has its steeply pitched "roof-wall," or mansard. The decorative motifs of a conventionalized running vine (*rinceau*) and incised squares doubtless were intended to remind art-lovers of the elegance of buildings of the Second Empire in France.

8. Leiter Building I. 1879.   L   II-B
(Later the Morris Building, now the 208 West Monroe Building.)
Architect: William L. Jenney.
208 West Monroe (100 S). Map 3.

The citation by the Landmarks Commission reads: "In recognition of its contribution towards the development of skeleton construction. Cast iron pilasters continue as columns from foundation to roof, with widely spaced piers forming glass bays, which anticipate the steel cage of the Chicago School." The floor beams are carried by cast-iron columns set against the brick piers of the facade, and thus the piers, relieved of part of their usual load, could be made narrower than would otherwise have been possible. The mullions (the narrower vertical members separating the individual windows) are also of cast iron. The aim of the architect in all this was not so much to develop any new style or conception of architectural effect, but simply to get more light into the offices.

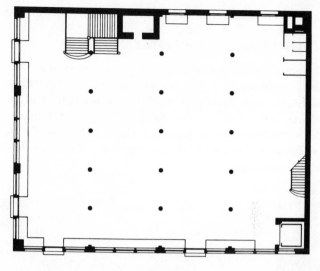

FIRST FLOOR

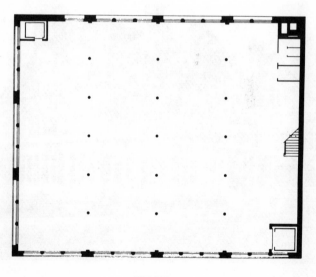

FIFTH FLOOR

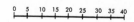

9. Florence Hotel (and Square). 1881. II-A
Architect: S. S. Beman.
11111 South Forestville (532 E). Map 1.

The hotel is a fascinating relic of the times, as vivid as some newly made set for a story of the eighties. The square and the houses near it preserve much of the atmosphere of the original town. Built by the Pullman Company for its employees and laid out by Beman, Pullman is historically important as an example of the contemporary ideas on village or city planning.

10. Hammond Library, Union Theological College. 1882.

I-A

Architects: Adler and Sullivan.

North Ashland (1600 W) and West Warren (34 N) (NW corner). Destroyed, 1963.

Long out of use and badly damaged, this building was razed in August, 1963. The decoration had a naïve and stiff quality, very different from the richness and flexibility of Sullivan's mature work. Perhaps some prophecy of his later mastery of design was to be found in the composition of the windows: they had a surprising variety within the generally unified effect gained through repetition of similar shapes. The little tower-like outlooks at the tops of the corner piers had an almost humorous charm.

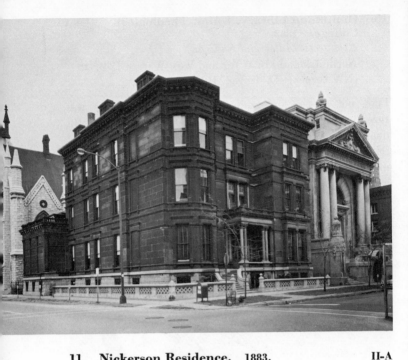

11. Nickerson Residence. 1883.   II-A
Architects: Burling and Whitehouse.
40 East Erie (658 N). Map 2.

One of the rich houses of the eighties and well preserved,
this classical structure, perhaps inspired by Parisian town-
houses, contrasts with Burling's more direct treatment of a
business building, as seen in the 200 West Adams Building
(No. 19). The interiors offer fascinating examples of the use
of period styles in such houses at the time. The owner was
one of the early art collectors of Chicago, and the Art Institute of Chicago now has in its collections works that doubtless appeared at one time in the "gallery" that formed a
part of this house.

12. Central Cold Storage Warehouse. 1883. II-A
(Originally the Hiram Sibley Warehouse.)
Architect: George H. Edbrooke.
315–31 North Clark (100 W). Map 3.

The design suggests the structural bay, i.e., the intervals between the supports. However, there are naïve touches of ornament, and even more naïve setting of piers or wall sections above mullions (the more slender vertical dividers). The river side was supported on thirty-foot oak piles, the first known use of deep piles under the wall of a building. Perhaps their use here was inspired by previous use of such piles under grain elevators along the river.

13. Fine Arts Building. 1884. IV
(Originally the Studebaker Building.)
Architect: S. S. Beman.
410 South Michigan (100 E). Map 3.

This building was long notable as a focus of Chicago's artistic life, because of the cultural events that took place in it and the artists who had studios in it. As features of the architectural composition, the two large columns in the third and fourth stories seem incongruous in the design, perhaps needing others to keep them company. The search for variety in the shapes and groupings of the windows is carried out along the same general lines as in the Auditorium (No. 20) next door, but this structure suffers from comparison with that more masterly design.

14. Glessner House. **1886.** **L   II-B**
(Now the Lithographic Technical Foundation.)
Architect: H. H. Richardson.
1800 South Prairie (300 E). Map 4.

The citation by the Landmarks Commission effectively sums
up the achievement in this wonderfully sturdy and solid
house: "In recognition of the fine planning for an urban
site, which opens the family rooms to the quiet serenity of
an inner yard; the effective ornament and decoration; and
the impressive Romanesque masonry, expressing dignity and
power." The north wall, with its powerful arch, is a fine
example of Richardson's handling of masonry and the only
surviving example in Chicago of the work of the greatest
American architect prior to the founding of the Chicago
School.

GLESSNER HOUSE

58

Window detail

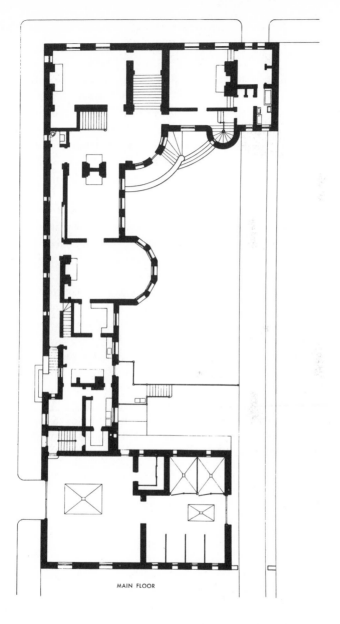

MAIN FLOOR

0 5 10 15 20 25 30

15. Rookery Building. 1886. L II-B
Architects: Burnham and Root.
209 South LaSalle (150 W). Map 3.

The citation by the Landmarks Commission reads: "In recognition of its pioneering plan in providing shops and offices around a graceful semi-private square and the further development of the skeleton structural frame using cast iron columns, wrought iron spandrel beams, and steel beams to support party walls and interior floors." (The ground story of the "court" was remodeled by Frank Lloyd Wright in 1905.)

A noteworthy combination of strength and grace is achieved in the design. The ornament is very interesting, especially its placement: in most cases it emphasizes architectural features, such as the floor lines within the larger openings, or the place where a capital might be; but in other cases it seems to be addressed simply, and courteously, to the spectator's enjoyment. The vigorous contrast of columns and heavy stonework is more effective and more unified than in the Fine Arts Building (No. 13). This contrast, the massive walls combined with large windows, the degree of emphasis at the corners, top, and center of the facade, all help to establish this building's strong presence. Root held that the virtues of architecture were similar to the traits of civilized people, and the Rookery can well be viewed in this way. It stands there like a stronghearted and cheerful person, forceful yet friendly.

ROOKERY BUILDING

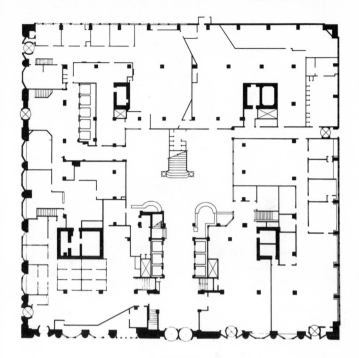

FIRST FLOOR

0 10 20 30 40

16.   St. Gabriel's Church.   1887.   II-B
Architects: Burnham and Root.
4501 South Lowe (632 W). Map 4.

This building is remarkable in the bold, broad massing of the chief elements, including the chapels at the back. The effect of breadth and strength is emphasized by the subtle batter (the inward slope of the wall as it rises), nicely worked out in the brick at the foot of the walls. The tower has been lowered by the removal of a section that was just below the present top story, and the latter has been rebuilt in line with the lower stories, whereas it originally projected beyond them. The tower has thus lost in force as well as in height. The present entrance porch has been added, and there are minor changes, as in the buttresses. The interior maintains its original breadth and spaciousness, owing to the broad vaulted shapes of the ceiling, although there has been some remodeling, especially in the northern part. Despite changes, the building still has a degree of individuality and character recalling the Rookery (No. 15), by the same architects.

17. Wirt Dexter Building. 1887. L II-B
(Now the 630 South Wabash Building.)
Architects: Adler and Sullivan.
630 South Wabash (45 E). Map. 3.

The narrow mullions, in the central bay, with the slight
moldings crossing them give a touch of distinction to the
otherwise very simple treatment of a commercial building.
(The central section originally ended in a low gable at the
top of the facade.) At the back is an interesting use of openwork iron members set outside the "wall," presumably to
conserve space inside.

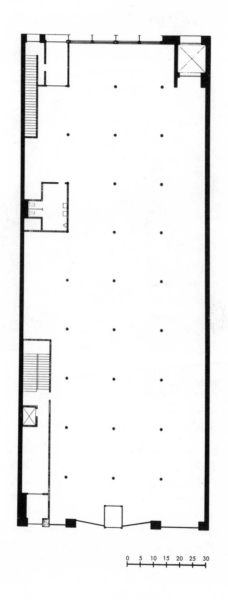

0 5 10 15 20 25 30

18. Willoughby Building. 1887.   II-B
(Now the 234 South Franklin Building.)
Architect: Leroy S. Buffington?
234 South Franklin (300 W). Map 3.

This building is said to have been designed by Buffington, the Minneapolis architect who claimed he "invented" the skyscraper. The use of iron columns and beams allows a considerable amount of window area and thus represents the approach to "skyscraper construction" found also in other buildings of the time, such as the earlier Leiter Building (No. 8). The architectural design, however, features numerous small and medium projections which produce an effect of fussiness rather than variety.

19. 200 West Adams Building. 1888.   II-B
Architects: Burling and Whitehouse.
200 West Adams (200 S). Map 3.

A sober, effective design for an office building, this represents the better commercial architecture of the time, comparing favorably, for instance, with Sullivan's design for the Wirt Dexter Building (No. 17). The slight rounding of the corners of the piers subtly emphasizes their mass.

73

20. Auditorium Building. 1889.   L   II-B
(Now Roosevelt University.)
Architects: Adler and Sullivan.
Michigan (100 E) and Congress (500 S)
(NW corner). Map 3.

One of Chicago's most famous cultural and architectural landmarks. The citation of the Landmarks Commission reads:
"In recognition of the community spirit which here joined
commercial and artistic ends, uniting hotel, office building,
and theatre in one structure; the inventiveness of the engineer displayed from foundations to the perfect acoustics;
and the genius of the architect which gave form and, with
the aid of original ornament, expressed the spirit of festivity
in rooms of great splendor."

The Auditorium is an American masterpiece that placed
Chicago building in the first rank. The bearing walls reveal
a powerful rhythm of limestone piers surmounting a rugged
granite base. Interior elements are carried on the most in-
tricate system of iron framing developed up to that time.
The theater is now being restored under the sponsorship of
the Auditorium Theater Council.

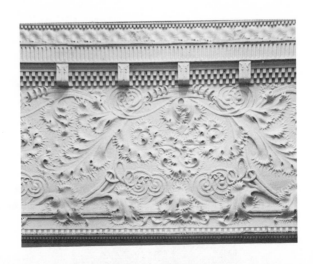

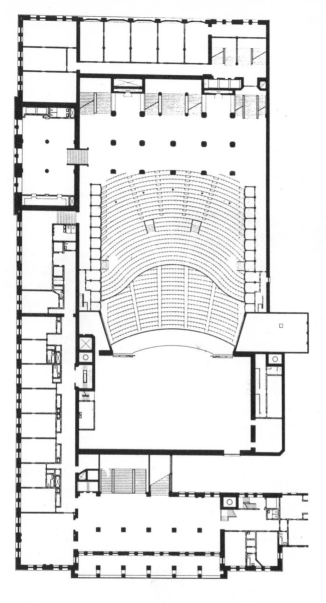

SECOND FLOOR

0 10 20 30 40

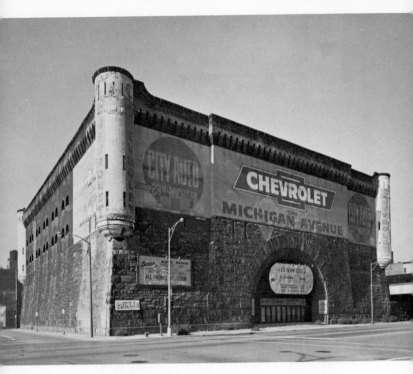

21. First Infantry Armory. 1890 (rebuilt 1894). **I-B**
(Later the 131st Infantry Armory.)
Architects: Burnham and Root.
South Michigan (100 E) and 16th (NW corner).
Map 4.

The military character of this building is clearly suggested
by the slight batter, or inward slope, of the lower walls, by
the large quarry-faced stone in which this part is carried
out, and finally by the simple imitation, at the top of the
building, of battlements and machicolations. (These latter are
openings, behind the battlements, through which in an earlier
day defenders could drop missiles or hot oil on the attackers
below.) Some of the stone on the east side has weathered
into fantastic forms, suggesting certain modern sculpture.

22. Manhattan Building. 1890. II-B
Architect: William L. Jenney.
431 South Dearborn (36 W). Map 3.

This and Burnham and Root's Rand McNally Building were
the first tall office buildings to use skeleton construction
throughout. Even the party walls are carried by the steel
frame, in this case on beams cantilevered out, i.e., extending
beyond their supporting columns. The building thus displays
Jenney's interest in structural matters and his inventiveness
in using the new material, iron or steel. The design, however,
is not particularly impressive. The various materials and the
different shapes in the bay windows, for instance, tend to
produce an effect of indecision.

23. Getty Tomb. 1890.   L   II-B

Graceland Cemetery.
Architect: Louis H. Sullivan.
4001 North Clark (100 W). Map 1.

The citation by the Landmarks Commission reads: "In recognition of the design which here brings new beauty to an age-old form: the tomb. Stone and bronze stand transformed in rich yet delicate ornament, a requiem for the dead, an inspiration to the living." The ornament cut on the stone is remarkable for the way in which an apparently routine geometrical motif, a spokelike figure inside an octagon, becomes, when repeated, a decoration of the greatest delicacy, like an openwork veil drawn over the solid stone. Aside from the scale and the degree of relief, which are fundamental, the execution of the "spokes" in successive series of small balls contributes a great deal to the delicacy and life of this ornament. The bronze doors contain some of Sullivan's finest ornament, with the spokelike motif of the stone ornament above subtly echoed within the rich floral design.

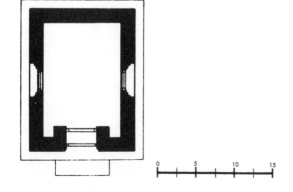

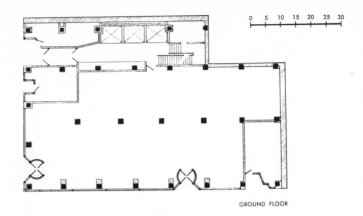

0 5 10 15 20 25 30

GROUND FLOOR

24. Reliance Building. 1895. L II-B
(Now the 32 North State Building.)
Architects: D. H. Burnham and Company.
32 North State. Map 3.

The citation by the Landmarks Commission reads: "In recognition of the early and complete expression, through slender piers, small spandrels, and the skillfully restrained use of terra cotta with large areas of glass, of the structural cage of steel that alone supports such buildings." The strength and convenience of steel construction were shown in the piecemeal manner in which this building was put up. In 1890 John Root designed a sixteen-story building for this site, but only the foundations and first story were built then. These were "slipped under" the upper stories of a four-story, heavy masonry building already there, the upper stories continuing in use during the process. In 1894 these older stories were "knocked off" and the present building carried on up. The designer in charge in 1894–95 was Charles Atwood, of D. H. Burnham and Company, who apparently redesigned the exteriors. It was at this time that the terra-cotta sheathing was designed. The moldings executed in the terra cotta accentuate the slenderness of the verticals and thus contribute to the sense of openness in the facades.

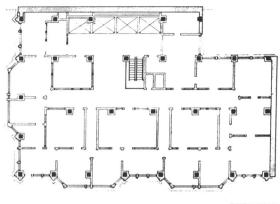

TYPICAL FLOOR

25. Grand Central Station. 1890. II-A
(Originally Wisconsin Central Station.)
Architect: S. S. Beman.
South Wells (200 W) and Harrison (600 S). Map 3.

The building is designed in a routine version of the Romanesque style. Architecturally it is noteworthy for the very fine tower. Structurally it is noted as the first building to be built entirely on long piles driven to a layer of stiff clay more than fifty feet below the surface. Despite the weight of the tower, this method prevented the uneven settling which was a serious problem for heavy buildings on the soft soil of Chicago (see No. 20). The train shed is interesting as an example of the glass and iron construction of the time, allowing maximum lightness and openness.

26. Sears, Roebuck and Company. 1891. **II-B**
   (Originally Leiter Building II.)
   Architects: Jenney and Mundie.
   State and Van Buren (400 S) (SE corner). Map 3.

An example of the "commercial style" for which Chicago
was famous. The piers are narrow enough to suggest the
metal frame within them, as do the slender piers and high
ceilings of the interior. Ornament is sparse, economy is suggested, and the general effect is simple and direct (more so
than in the slightly later Fair Building, by the same architects, on the NW corner at State and Adams).

27. Monadnock Building. 1891.   L   II-B
Architects: Burnham and Root.
53 West Jackson (300 S). Map 3.

The citation by the Landmarks Commission reads: "In recognition of its original design and its historical interest as the highest wall-bearing structure in Chicago. Restrained use of brick, soaring massive walls, omission of ornamental forms, unite in a building simple yet majestic." The extreme thickness of the walls (six feet at ground level) showed that to go higher in traditional masonry construction was not feasible; the time had come for the introduction of iron, and then steel, as the essential materials for tall buildings. Noteworthy is the movement given to the walls by the curvature inward above the first story and out again at the top, with the corners "chamfered" off.

MONADNOCK BUILDING

GROUND FLOOR   TYPICAL FLOOR

28. The Art Institute. 1892. IV

Architects: Shepley, Rutan and Coolidge.
Michigan (100 E) at Adams (200 S). Map 3.

Chief home of the visual arts in Chicago, the building, like many museums of its time, was inspired by the architectural tradition of the Renaissance, as taught in the Ecole des Beaux Arts in Paris, and is thus frankly traditional in character. The McKinlock Court, built in 1924 in the eastern enlargement, Coolidge and Hodgson architects, is a pleasant oasis of classicism. Here lunch is served in the open air in summer. The classical arcades of the court are not quite overwhelmed by the rout of sea creatures in the fountain by Carl Milles. (This fountain, set up in 1931, is a duplicate of one in Lidingo, Sweden.)

29. Charnley House. 1892.   L   II-B
Architects: Adler and Sullivan; Frank Lloyd Wright.
1365 North Astor (50 E). Map 2.

Officially by the firm of Adler and Sullivan, this house is
believed to have been designed by Wright while in their
employ. The closed-up, blocky design is in marked contrast
to Wright's later "prairie" houses (see No. 57). The shallow
brick and the cut stone are the background for the very
formal design, of which the obvious elements are the door
and the small windows. The balcony, in its lightness and
openness, contrasts with the solid mass of the house. Despite
its shallowness, one may ask whether it perhaps puts an
excessive emphasis on the center of a short facade (contrast
No. 33). A later extension of the facade to the right, in the
porches built there, obscures its original symmetry.

FIRST FLOOR

SECOND FLOOR

THIRD FLOOR

0 5 10 15 20 25 30

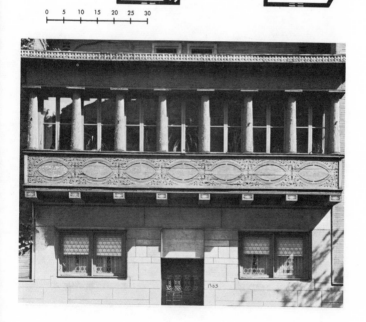

30. Fortnightly Club. 1892. II-A

(Originally the Lathrop House.)
Architects: McKim, Mead and White.
120 East Bellevue (1031 N). Map 2.

An unusually fine facade in the classic manner, related to the Georgian style of the eighteenth century. The shallow relieving arches over the openings of the first floor, the scale of the decoration over the three central ones, the relative emphasis in the two string courses and the cornice, and the vigor given by the projection of the ample bays at each end are the most obvious features of a masterly design, clear, open, urbane. In part because of the placing of the door, the facade carries its symmetry easily, without rigidity or undue emphasis. The length of the central window of the third floor, which breaks the string course below the other windows here, was related to a light, openwork balcony outside it, now removed; similar balconies were outside the three central windows of the second floor.

31. Newberry Library. 1892. IV
Architect: Henry I. Cobb.
60 West Walton (932 N). Map 2.

Housing one of the great research collections of the Midwest, the building was built to the specifications of a strong-minded librarian who insisted on such features as hallways constructed almost as separate buildings, in order to preserve quiet in the reading rooms. The massive, Romanesque style follows H. H. Richardson's example and was used by Cobb in several other buildings of Chicago and vicinity, such as the former home of the Chicago Historical Society (later the Institute of Design, now the Studio Building, 632 North Dearborn).

32. Garrick Building. 1892. L II-B
(Originally the Schiller Building.)
Architects: Adler and Sullivan.
64 West Randolph (150 N). Destroyed, 1961.

A combined theater and office building, the theater occupied the ground floor and up to part of the seventh story, the rest of the building being devoted to offices. The superb tower had a wonderful upward movement, emphasized by the way the piers "cut through" the horizontals. Here, in contrast to the purely commercial Meyer Building (No. 34), the artistic purpose was given very obvious emphasis by liberal use of Sullivan's rich ornament at the top and bottom of the building and in the interior of the auditorium. (The foundations rested on long piles, driven fifty feet to hard clay, and thus the weight of the tower created no difficulties.)

0 5 10 15 20 25 30

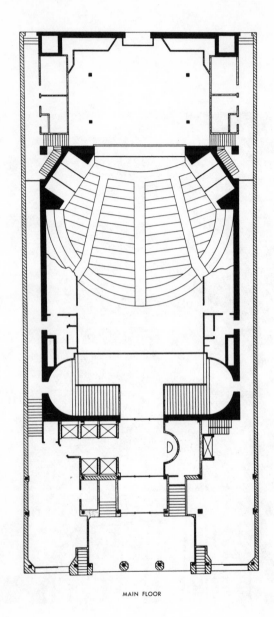

MAIN FLOOR

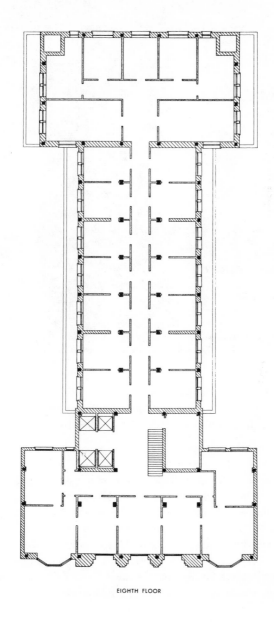

EIGHTH FLOOR

33. Sullivan House. 1892. L II-B
Architects: Adler and Sullivan.
4575 South Lake Park (about 1200 E). Map 4.

A noteworthy example of a city house by Adler and Sullivan. The blocky character of the stone facade is similar to that of the Charnley House (No. 29), and, since Wright apparently designed the domestic structures for the firm, it is possible that the design is his. The rich ornament over the door suggests Sullivan. Other ornamentation on the facade was removed by vandals in 1964. Louis Sullivan lived in this house during part of the nineties, the high point of his architectural career. It is now occupied by a volunteer welfare group, which has undertaken to rehabilitate it.

34. Meyer Building. 1893. L   II-B
Architects: Adler and Sullivan.
307 West Van Buren (400 S). Map 4.

At first one notices only the simple form, suggesting prac-
ticality, blocklike except for the projecting cornice (now
removed) and the strange column-like mullions (dividers,
thinner than piers, in the window areas). However, this
building deserves closer study, for one will find in the design many interesting and subtle decisions made by the
designer. The horizontals are given slightly greater emphasis than the verticals, by their greater width and by the
strips of restrained ornament that cross the piers at the sill
lines and the heads of the windows. There is a slight projection at the "top" of the piers in each story, not strong
enough to be called a capital but giving a subtle emphasis,
in a somewhat traditional manner, to the pier where it meets
the horizontal strip of wall. This particular horizontal accent is omitted on the corner piers (although a narrow band
of ornament crosses them), perhaps because of the designer's
feeling that there should be less interruption of the vertical
movement in these piers. Such decisions have nothing to
do with the structure, or even with the function, but are
part of a more general aesthetic element which, in one way
or another, distinguishes architecture as art from mere
building.

35. Yondorf Building. 1892. II-B
(Now the 225–29 South Wacker Building.)
Architect unknown.
225–29 South Wacker (formerly South Market)
(360 W). Map 3.

This building has an amazing lightness and openness for
a structure said to have been built originally in 1874. The
"remodeling" of 1892 in reality must have been a rebuild-
ing. The slender brick verticals between the windows are too
narrow to support themselves and thus suggest to the spectator the presence of iron or steel in addition to brick.

36. The Old Chicago Stock Exchange. 1894. L II-B
(Now the 30 North LaSalle Building.)
Architects: Adler and Sullivan.
30 North LaSalle (150 W). Map 3.

The treatment of the wall above the third story is noteworthy, the facets of the projecting bays making an effective
contrast with the plane of the wall, which is emphasized by
the larger windows and their framing strips. The proportions of the design have been criticized, for instance, for the
great height of the "base," which includes three stories.
Doubtless Sullivan wished to consider the trading room a
part of the "base," since this important room was reached by
a stairway directly from the street level. It was on the second
floor and was two stories high. The tall arches which link the
second- and third-floor windows thus "express" this high
room (although it was in the center of the building and not
immediately behind these windows). The running pattern of
the ornament just above the arches has a wonderful move-

ment in its curving forms, and its flat surface makes it admirably suited to a wall. Perhaps the entrance piece breaks uncomfortably into the second- and third-story band, but the arch itself is majestic. (The relief in the left-hand medallion represents the house of P. F. W. Peck, 1837, which originally stood on this site; the right-hand medallion contains the year in which the present building was begun, 1893.)

The first "caisson" foundations in Chicago were used under the west wall of this building. They were devised by General Sooy Smith, an engineer who was the chief authority on foundations in Chicago at this time. These caissons consisted of deep wells sunk here to hard clay, the sides of the wells being held in place by wood sheathing and steel rings until they were filled with concrete. They thus supported the building in the same manner as the long wood piles that had been used elsewhere (see No. 25), but they avoided the shock and vibration caused to immediately adjacent buildings by the driving of the long piles.

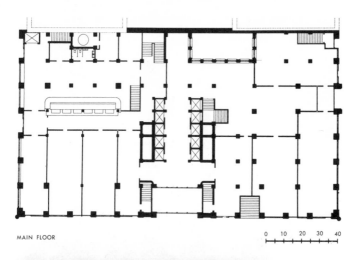

MAIN FLOOR

0   10   20   30   40

37. Francis Apartments. 1895.   L   II-B
Architect: Frank Lloyd Wright.
4304 South Forestville (532 E). Map 4.

This apartment building is an interesting example of Wright's early work. In character it has the simple blockiness of the Charnley House (No. 29). The balconies on the facade offer a striking illustration of the effect of relationships on individual forms. If we look at only one of the wings, the balcony seems to be an excessive emphasis on the center of a short facade; but when the two wings are seen together, the balconies take their places as quite acceptable emphases on either side of the deep penetration of the "court" between the wings. The ornament is a very interesting simplification of Sullivan's more complex type.

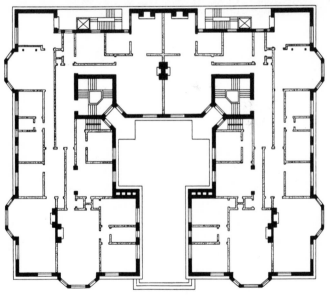

TYPICAL FLOOR

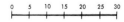

0   5   10   15   20   25   30

38. Francisco Terrace Apartments. 1895.   II-B
    Architect: Frank Lloyd Wright.
    253–57 North Francisco (2900 W). Map 1.

Wright's answer to the problem of the lower-priced apartment building at this time. Although he omits the extensive
ornament of the Francis Apartments (No. 37), even here
the artist appears, as in the purely aesthetic paneling of the
brick on the west front, which, however, does not detract
from the monumental dignity and simplicity of this low-
cost housing. The strange single column in the occasional
short windows recalls the column-like mullions of the Meyer
Building (No. 34).

39.   Marquette Building.   1895.   II-B
  Architects: Holabird and Roche.
  140 South Dearborn (36 W). Map 3.

Despite the conventional cornice, the Marquette is one of
the least old-fashioned in appearance and still one of the
finest office buildings in Chicago. Top and bottom follow
Sullivan's idea of setting off the first two and the topmost
stories from the others—with the addition here of a transi-
tional story, as it were, in each case. The fine proportions
of the windows, the vigorous projection of the piers, and
the effective simple patterning of the piers of the end bays
combine to give the building its strong yet pleasing character. The very end bay on Adams Street is a later addition
1905, and outside the original design. The bronze reliefs
above the entrance, by American sculptor Hermon A. Mac-
Neil, portray incidents from the life of Père Marquette.

116

40. Fisher Building. 1896.
  Architects: D. H. Burnham and Company.
  343 South Dearborn (36 W). Map 3.

An early example of the application of Gothic style to the skyscraper. The detail is consistently Gothic in inspiration, and the corner piers are even given the form of Gothic piers with engaged colonnettes (or moldings). One may note the emphasis on height which this accomplishes, aided here by the verticals of the projecting bays. The design achieves a notable openness and lightness, hardly inferior to the Reliance Building (No. 24), and thus vigorously expresses the steel frame despite the presence of the historical detail.

118

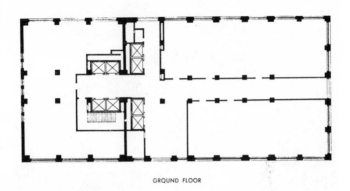

GRQUND FLOOR

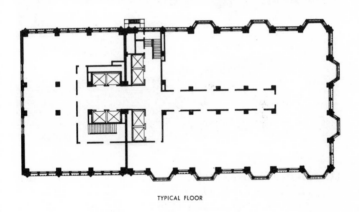

TYPICAL FLOOR

119

41. Heller House. 1897.   **L   II-B**
Architect: Frank Lloyd Wright.
5132 South Woodlawn (1200 E). Map 5.

A notable example of Wright's work at this time. Still quite
blocklike and closed up below, like many of his earlier
houses, it is more open on the upper floor and shows a more
interesting silhouette than the Charnley House (No. 29).
The lightening and opening of the upper part foreshadows
his later designs. The molded plaster frieze at the top is by
sculptor Richard Bock.

120

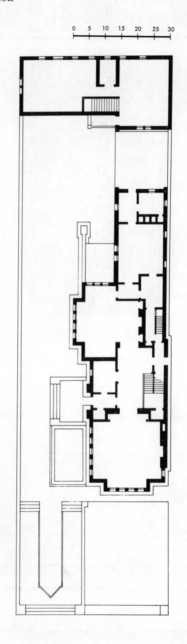

42. 731 South Plymouth Building. 1897. II-B
(Originally the Lakeside Press Building.)
Architect: Howard V. Shaw.
731 South Plymouth (31 W). Map 3.

A vigorous design of generally traditional character, but
freely treated so that it seems original rather than imitative.
The facade gains interest from the way the arches over
some of the openings are played off against the flat heads,
or lintels, of others and the greater openness of the upper
stories against the greater solidity of the lower two. The
spandrels (horizontal strips of wall at the floor levels) in
the upper stories, and the window glass throughout, are set
well back from the surfaces of the piers so as to show their
mass, which contributes greatly to the vigor and strength
of the whole design. The centerpiece, around the doors, is
interesting in its modifications of classical motifs. The coat-
of-arms, with its Indian head and the representation of Fort
Dearborn in relief, and the medallions refer to series of
books published by the Lakeside Press.

43. Gage Building. 1898. L II-B
Architects: Holabird and Roche. Louis H. Sullivan.
18 South Michigan (100 E). Map 3.

Only the facade was designed by Sullivan. The citation by the Landmarks Commission refers to it: "In recognition of the fine relations established between piers, windows, and wall surfaces; the excellence of proportions throughout; and the imaginative use of original ornament." Sometimes Sullivan's ornament seems plastered on at spots, rather than integrated with a building, and the two bursts of ornament at the tops of the piers suggest as much, in this instance. Note, however, that the architect designed an eight-story facade, the other four stories being added later, in 1902. Comparison of photographs taken before and after suggests, surprisingly, that these ornaments were perhaps "held in" better in the smaller facade. There was also a band of rich, though more delicate, ornament along the top of the first story, which probably helped. The two buildings to the south, 30 and 24 South Michigan, were done entirely by Holabird and Roche. Their facades form an interesting contrast with the facade of the Gage Building. The basic design is the same, but they do not have the refinement and elegance of proportion and accent to be found in the Gage. In their avoidance of ornament they seem to look to the future more directly than does Sullivan's design.

GAGE BUILDING

126

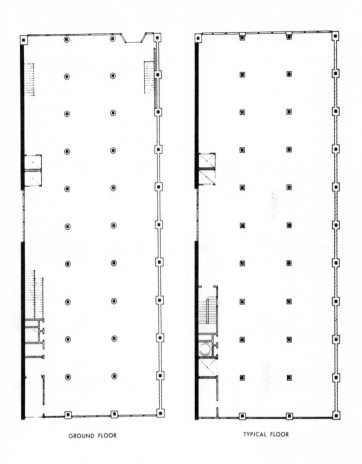

GROUND FLOOR   TYPICAL FLOOR

0   10   20   30   40

44. Cable Building. 1899.
Architects: Holabird and Roche.
57 East Jackson (300 S). Destroyed, 1961.

A good example of the standard reached in the best average practice by the end of the century. Save for some classical details, especially at the cornice, the "style" was quite modern. The grouping of the windows and the vertical piers running strongly through the horizontals recalled the Gage Building, but without quite the refinement of design found there. See No. 86 for the successor building on this site.

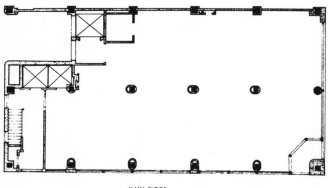

MAIN FLOOR

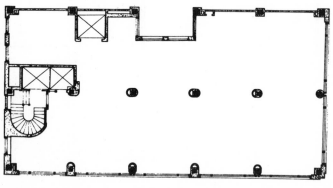

TYPICAL FLOOR

45. Carson Pirie Scott Store. 1899, 1903-4.   L   II-B
(Originally the Schlesinger and Mayer Store.)
Architect: Louis H. Sullivan.
State and Madison (SE corner). Map 3.

The easternmost section of three bays on Madison Street was
built first, and the main section, extending around the corner and with seven bays on State Street, several years later.
(The third section was done by D. H. Burnham and Company in 1906, and the southernmost by Holabird and Root
in 1960–61.) The fine proportions of the window openings,
the firm emphasis in the moldings around them, the accent
given by the line of delicate ornament on the horizontal wall
sections, the deep window reveals, all provide a powerful
statement of iron and steel framing and contribute to a perfection of design rarely to be found. The rich ornament of
the first and second floors has been criticized as too ornate
for a commercial building. However, one should note that
Sullivan held that the display windows were like pictures and
deserved rich frames, and his prophetic power is seen in this,
if one compares old photographs showing the stodgy displays
of the time with the window-dressers' art of today. The citation by the Landmarks Commission reads: "In recognition
of the fine expression of interior spaces in the serene horizontals of window and wall; the execution of an original
system of ornament, and the excellent craftsmanship of its
execution in cast-iron."

As in many of the older buildings, the original projection,
or cornice, at the top has been replaced by a bald parapet.
The large festoons of ornament which were originally set
outside the piers between the first and second floors have
also been removed. (One wonders whether they could ever
have seemed very closely related to the wall, rather than
"hung on" it.) They contained the initials "SM" for the
owners. The architect's initials "LHS" can still be seen in
some of the ornament, perhaps slipped in by George G.
Elmslie, who, as Sullivan's chief designer, carried out much
of the ornamental design.

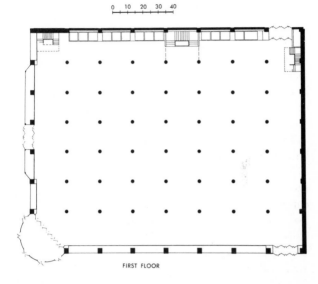

FIRST FLOOR

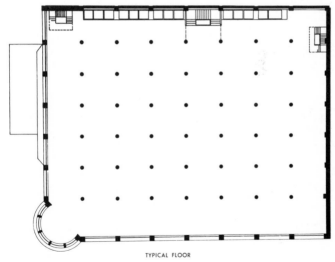

TYPICAL FLOOR

46.   The Coliseum.   1900.   I-B
Architects: Frost and Granger.
Engineers: E. C. and R. M. Shankland.
1513 South Wabash (45 E). Map 4.

A building of varied associations: the Republican National
Convention met in it from 1904 to 1920; many notables of
society were regularly seen here at the annual horse show,
including occasional out-of-town visitors such as Alice
Roosevelt and J. P. Morgan; whereas very different strata
of society paraded under its great arches at the First Ward
Ball, held here for many years.

The architecture itself is almost equally varied. The strange
battlemented sections on Wabash Avenue are the remains of
a wall built in 1889 around Libby Prison! (The prison had
been removed from Richmond, Virginia, by a group of
enterprising promoters and re-erected here as a Civil War
memento and museum, standing on this site from 1889 until
1899.) In the present building, of 1900, the twelve great
arches, three-hinged trusses in design, which cover the large
area without interior supports, recall the development of
construction in iron and steel of the nineteenth century.
(These arches collapsed during construction, killing eleven
workmen, apparently because of lack of care on the part of
the construction gangs, since when re-erected they held
securely.) The task of Charles S. Frost and his partner, the
architects, was hardly more than to put a shell around the
engineers' trusses. In doing this they were perhaps inspired
by recollection of the exterior of ancient Roman vaulted
buildings.

135

47. Crown Building. 1900.   L   II-B
(Originally the McClurg Building.)
Architects: Holabird and Roche.
218 South Wabash (45 E). Map 3.

Remarkable for the light and open character of the facade.
A fascinating study of design, for instance, the relative
emphasis on the horizontal versus the vertical and on openness versus solidness, is offered by comparison of the treatment of the wall in this building with that in the Marquette
Building (No. 39) and the Carson Pirie Scott Store (No.
45). The three also offer interesting comparisons of the
treatment of the "Chicago windows," that is, windows in
which a fixed center light or lights are flanked by movable
sashes at the sides.

0   10   20   30   40

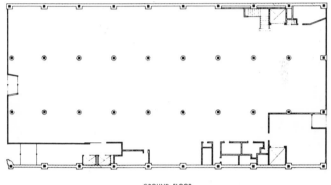

GROUND FLOOR

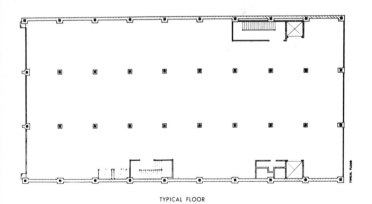

TYPICAL FLOOR

137

48. Schoenhofen Brewery Building. 1902. L   II-B
(Now the Morningstar-Paisley Company.)
Architects: Richard E. Schmidt; Hugh Garden.
West 18th and Canalport (1800 S)
(NE corner). Map 4.

An interesting example of the work of the group of architects who were developing a non-historical approach at the
beginning of the century. In this building there is a fine
appreciation of the qualities of brick and considerable inventiveness in attaining accents or emphases by the way it
is laid. Although Schmidt was the commissioned architect,
the design was apparently made by Hugh Garden, who was
occasionally retained by Schmidt for a given design before
1906, the year they formed a partnership.

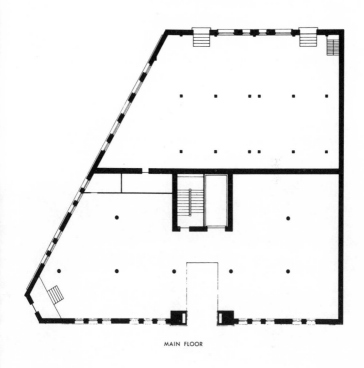

MAIN FLOOR

0   5   10   15   20   25   30

49. **Madlener House.** 1902.   **L**   **II-B**
(Now the Graham Foundation for
Advanced Studies in the Fine Arts.)
Architect: Richard E. Schmidt.
4 West Burton (1500 N). Map 2.

A clear, cubical mass, as forceful as a Florentine palace.
There is an interesting variety in the various emphases on
the horizontal, in stone base, string courses, and grouping
of the windows. The decoration around the door is a fine
piece of modern ornament, similar to Sullivan's geometric
type. The interior has been remodeled and restored for the
Graham Foundation by Brenner, Danforth and Rockwell.

50. Holy Trinity Russian Orthodox Cathedral. 1903.   II-A
Architect: Louis H. Sullivan.
1121 North Leavitt (2200 W). Map 1.

Interesting as a work in a traditional form by the "prophet
of modern architecture." The basic form is that of Russian
churches, derived from the earlier Byzantine architecture.
The plan is a central type, basically a square with extensions
at ground level, the central space crowned with a dome. In
the interior the proportions of the space—small, but with
relatively large arches—the painted decoration, and the shallow dome combine to produce an effect of delicacy and refinement, as of a richly decorated coffer or jewel box. The
exterior is simple, with occasional exotic touches in curved
shapes or angular window hoods. The exotic becomes more
obvious in the onion-like shape above the lantern, which
must be inspired by the bulbous domes found in Russian
church architecture. Ornament is very sparingly used, the
most striking appearance being in the cut-out ornament in
wood over the entrance, similar to that originally in the interior of the Carson Pirie Scott Store (No. 45).

141

51. Chapin and Gore Building. 1904.   **L**   **II-B**
(Later the Nepeenauk Building, now the 63 East
Adams Building.)
Architect: Richard E. Schmidt.
63 East Adams (200 S). Map 3.

There is an originality almost mannerist here, as in the
split window-framing panels on the second floor, contrasting with the beautifully simple piers above; these piers then
flowered at the top into the "upside-down capitals," as they
were called when first seen. Unfortunately they have been removed. Also the original cornice has been replaced with a
parapet, and this, with the absence of the original capitals,
makes the upper part of the building incongruously bare in
relation to the lower part.

142

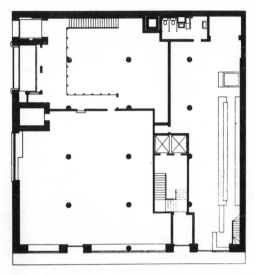

MAIN FLOOR

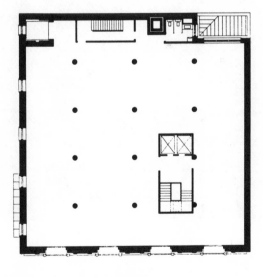

TYPICAL FLOOR

143

52. E-Z Polish Building. 1905. **L II-B**
(Now the Universal Foods Corporation.)
Architect: Frank Lloyd Wright.
3005 West Carroll (338 N). Map 1.

Little remains of the original design here. The building has
been enlarged, the windows filled up, and the original open
stair-towers at the ends closed. The interior has been remodeled and the original surfaces covered.

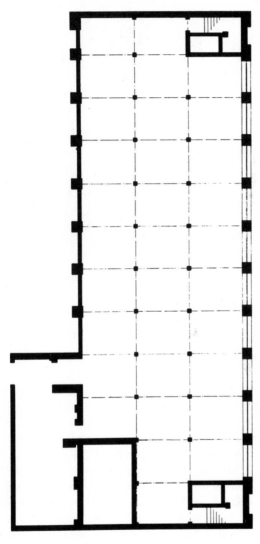

BASEMENT FLOOR

53. Magerstadt House. 1906.   L   II-B
Architect: George W. Maher.
4930 South Greenwood (1100 E). Map 5.

A design by one of the architects who were co-workers or
assistants of Frank Lloyd Wright. Very shallow brick, with
subtle emphasis by projection here and there, is used in a
design which consistently emphasizes a more massive quality than is found in Wright's contemporary houses. Perhaps,
too, there is more obvious recollection of other styles: the
profile of the cornice of the porch and the small rectangular
blocks or "dentils" under it remind one of classical forms,
and the foliate ornament on the capitals of the columns
perhaps recalls the Art Nouveau decoration at the turn of
the century. The long plan and the entrance at the side of
the city lot will be found in Wright's Robie House (No. 57);
however, the frame around the entrance is more massive
and less integrated with the rest of the building than in
Wright's famous work.

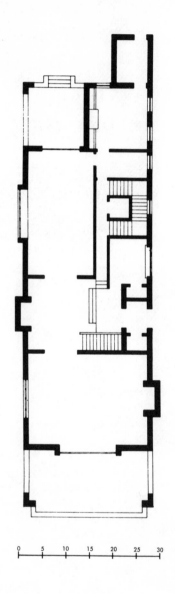

0   5   10   15   20   25   30

54. Montgomery Ward and Company Warehouse. 1907.
II-B

Architects: Schmidt, Garden and Martin.
618 West Chicago (800 N). Map 1.

A warehouse which attains conscious and distinct architectural quality. An enormous and massive structure is given life by the movement in the spandrels (horizontal wall sections) accented by the projecting strips at top and bottom. (Brick facing on these sections accentuated their horizontal form in contrast to the piers, but they have lost this effect through being painted.) One should not overlook the ornament, a rosette-like form at the top of the verticals, and a swordlike motif at the top of the second story. The sober effect of strength is a good expression of the reinforced concrete construction. (The calculations for the loads carried in the structure were taken by Richard Schmidt from German technical publications with which he was familiar, since a reinforced concrete frame of this type had not been used before this by Chicago architects.)

55. Our Lady of Lebanon Church. 1908.   L   II-B
(Originally the First Congregational
Church of Austin.)
Architects: Guenzel and Drummond.
Waller (5700 W) and Midway Park (500 N). Map 1.

Standing in what was originally the suburb of Austin, this church is a fine example of the work of the Chicago School, some of whose members, as in this case, are almost forgotten. Through the fine composition of rectangular masses in brick, the nave, or central part of the interior, is well expressed, as are also the lower side aisles. Without the ingenuity, or the complicated character, of Wright's Unity Temple in Oak Park, the interior is spacious and serene, and can bear comparison very well.

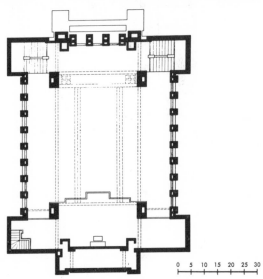

56. Liberty Mutual Insurance Building. 1908. II-B
(Originally the Hunter Building.) L
Architect: Christian A. Eckstrom.
337 West Madison. Map 3.

This building represents the typical level of achievement in the office building, as carried on by many architects. Here there are direct expression of the skeleton frame of steel and the suggestion of plenty of light in the offices. However, the way in which the building continues above the cornice at the top of the tenth story is disconcerting, as if the projected height had been changed during the construction. The variation in quality in these generally satisfactory buildings is seen by comparing the Dwight Building (No. 60), which has a design of the same general character.

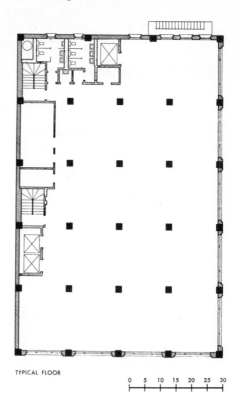

TYPICAL FLOOR

0   5   10   15   20   25   30

153

SECOND FLOOR

THIRD FLOOR

57. Robie House. 1909.   **L   II-B**
Architect: Frank Lloyd Wright.
5757 South Woodlawn (1200 E). Map 5.

One of the most famous houses in the world. It shows the
perfected type of the so-called prairie house, adapted here
to a narrow city lot; in its own right it must rate as
one of the most brilliant designs in the history of architecture. The citation by the Landmarks Commission reads: "In
recognition of the creation of the Prairie House—a home
organized around a great hearth where interior space, under
wide sweeping roofs, opens to the outdoors. The bold inter-
play of horizontal planes about the chimney mass, and the
structurally expressive piers and windows, established a new
form of domestic design." In 1963 the Robie House was
designated as a Registered National Historic Landmark.

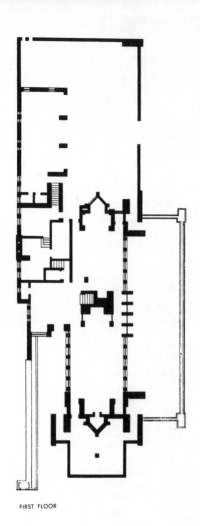

FIRST FLOOR

0   5   10 15 20 25 30 35 40

ROBIE HOUSE

58. Carl Schurz High School. 1909.   **L   II-B**
Architect: Dwight H. Perkins.
Milwaukee at Addison (3600 N). Map 1.

A dramatic composition of rising verticals in the walls, suddenly stopped by the deep overhangs of high-pitched roofs set at varying levels. A very strong string course at the top of the first floor echoes the roof line. The building is fortunate in having sufficient space around it to allow for it to be seen clearly.

CARL SCHURZ HIGH SCHOOL

158

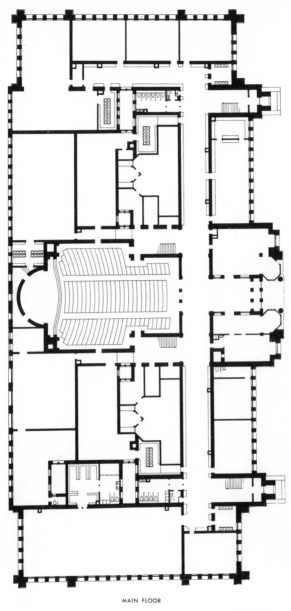

MAIN FLOOR

0 10 20 30 40

**59. Grover Cleveland Elementary School.   L   II-B
1910.**
Architect: Dwight H. Perkins.
3850 North Albany (3100 W). Map 1.

Another example of the work of Perkins, who to some degree
specialized in school architecture. Less varied and dramatic
than his Carl Schurz School (No. 58), it is a strong and
severe design, the chief forms emphasized by borders of
contrasting brick. The piers terminate in an interesting
capital block, which makes an effective transition to the wall
above. (By a curious optical illusion these piers seem wider
at the second and third stories than at the first, perhaps because of their lighter color.)

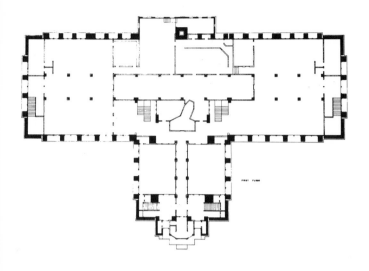

FIRST FLOOR

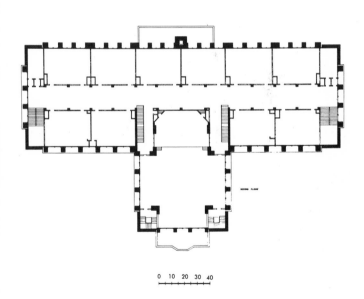

SECOND FLOOR

0 10 20 30 40

161

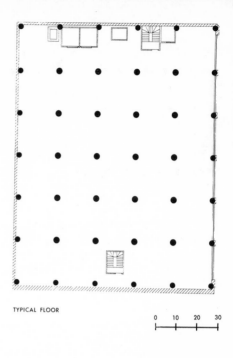

TYPICAL FLOOR

0   10   20   30

60. Dwight Building. 1911.   L   II-B
   Architects: Schmidt, Garden and Martin.
   626 South Clark (100 W). Map 3.

This building shows the application of the general principles
of design seen in the Montgomery Ward Warehouse (No.
54) to an office building. Similar framing strips can be
seen on the horizontals but here are limited to the upper edge
of these members. Hardly interrupting the upward movement of the wall, these accents distinguish the sills from the
heads of the windows and emphasize the agreeable horizontal
proportions of the windows themselves. An instructive comparison can be made with the Hunter Building (No. 56);
note the more decisive ending of the design at the top and the
generally greater distinction in the proportions and divisions
of the windows in the Dwight Building.

162

61. Edison Shop. 1912.   **L   II-B**
(Now Hung Fa Village Restaurant.)
Architects: Purcell, Feick and Elmslie.
229 South Wabash (45 E). Map 3.

One of the finest attempts to transform the facade of the
smaller commercial building into something more friendly
and intimate than usual. The citation by the Landmarks
Commission reads: "In recognition of its distinctive design;
the opening of the facade is welcome; the use of planting;
thus humanizing the commercial shop, making it a place of
dignity and beauty." The lower floor has been remodeled,
closing up the original courtlike entrance space, bamboo
has been added, and thus much of the original charm has
been lost. The upper stories of the facade remain as originally designed.

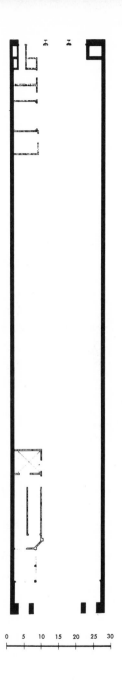

0   5   10   15   20   25   30

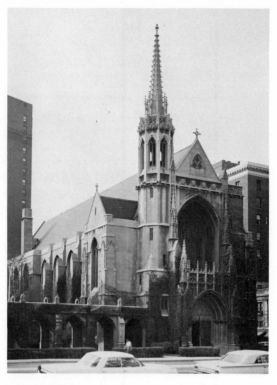

62.   Fourth Presbyterian Church   II-A
and Parish House.   1912.
Architects: Ralph A. Cram; Howard V. Shaw.
126 East Chestnut (860 N). Map 2.

The church is by one of the leaders of the Gothic revival in
the United States, Ralph A. Cram, and the accurate knowl-
edge of the Gothic style found in this building contrasts with
the more naïve imitation in such earlier buildings as Holy
Family (No. 4) or the Water Tower (No. 5). However, the
Gothic features are often modified, as in the narrowness of
the side aisles, the shape of the piers, and the use of the
transept space for a balcony, suggesting that the architect
allowed himself some degree of freedom. The severity of the
exterior contrasts with the warmer and more varied wall surfaces in the adjacent Parish House by Howard V. Shaw.

63. City of Chicago   L   II-B
Central Office Building. **1913.**
(Originally Reid, Murdock and Company.)
Architect: George C. Nimmons.
325 North LaSalle (150 W). Map 3.

This structure is typical of a number of buildings designed
by Nimmons for commercial or manufacturing use. It is
simple and straightforward, although with some traditional
feeling, as in the massiveness emphasized at points here.
The brick is used very effectively for its texture and pattern, finely set off by terra-cotta accents. The building is
now well maintained and gives a good idea of the original,
although it has been remodeled, one bay having been removed from its west side when LaSalle Street was widened.

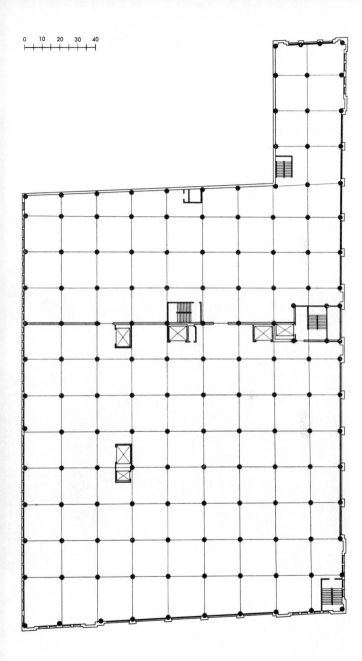

64. Park Buildings, Fuller Park. 1915. II-B
Architect: Edward H. Bennett.
45th and South Princeton (300 W). Map 4.

Interesting for the inventive use of concrete for texture and pattern, as in the waffle-like areas, or for forms inspired by classic architecture but carried out in concrete, as in the pilasters, or decorative strips, at the sides of the large windows. The planning is clear and spacious: note the enlivening of the space of the entrance vestibule of the main building by the niches. The links connecting the gymnasiums to the main building have been remodeled, the roofs of each link having had originally a small gable echoing those on the front of the main building.

65.   Wrigley Building. 1921, 1924.   IV
Architects: Graham, Anderson, Probst and White.
North Michigan (100 E) at the River (north bank).
Map 3.

The first of the celebrated skyscraper group at Michigan and
the River, the Wrigley represents an unabashed adaptation
of Baroque ornament to the screenlike walls of the high
framed building. Behind the thin screen that unites the main
building and its annex is a handsome little plaza with planting and fountain nicely scaled to the narrow area.

66. Krause Music Store. 1922.   L   II-B
(Now the Arntzen-Coleman Company.)
Architects: Louis H. Sullivan; William C. Presto.
4611 North Lincoln (about 2300 W). Map 1.

Sullivan's last work, and still typical, in the restrained ornament in the recess of the facade and the sensitive patterning
of the upper wall, of his best work. On the other hand, the
three large ornamental forms up and down the center line of
the facade seem hung on rather than integrated with the design as a whole. They overwhelm the little facade, which is
far too short to carry such an emphatic central emphasis.

FIRST FLOOR

67. Tribune Tower. 1925. IV
Architects: Hood and Howells.
North Michigan (100 E) at the River (north bank).
Map 3.

Familiar to the general public as the home of the *Chicago Tribune* and among architects and students of architecture as the winning design in an international competition held by the *Tribune* in 1922. Although this Gothic revival design won first place, the wide discussion of the award led to general agreement that the modern office building, or skyscraper, should be designed in a modern style. The discussion has obscured some of the virtues which, modern or not, this building has, such as the active and picturesque silhouette and the interesting treatment of the wall, with vertical sections of different widths. The simpler brick structure just east of and joined to the Tower was built as a separate building, the Tribune Plant, and designed by architect Jarvis Hunt.

68. Rockefeller Memorial Chapel. 1928.   II-A
    Architect: Bertram W. Goodhue.
    59th at Woodlawn (1200 E). Map 5.

An impressive example of the later Gothic revival by one of
its leading practitioners in the United States. Its massive and
solid character contrasts with the lighter quality of the
Fourth Presbyterian Church (No. 62) by Goodhue's former
partner, Ralph A. Cram.

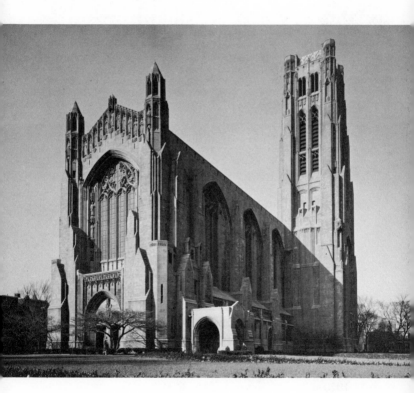

69.　Merchandise Mart.　1929-30.　　　　　**IV**
Architects: Graham, Anderson, Probst and White.
The River (north bank) between Wells (200 W)
and Orleans (340 W). Map 3.

Notable for years (until the Pentagon was built in Washington, D.C.) as the world's largest building (in floor area about four million square feet). It is also notable as one of the sites of the "markets" of furniture and furnishings, attended by buyers from all over the country, in which new offerings are displayed in showrooms maintained by manufacturers. The style is the skyscraper verticalism of the late 1920's.

70. Palmolive Building. 1929-30.
Architects: Holabird and Root.
919 North Michigan (100 E). Map 2.

One of the first skyscrapers in Chicago to adopt the simplified vertical style, it contrasts with the Tribune (No. 67) and others treated in historical styles. It achieves a lively silhouette of rising masses by its use of setbacks. A familiar sight to Chicagoans is its Lindbergh Beacon, which serves as a guide to airplanes.

71. Third Unitarian Church. 1937. L II-B
Architect: Paul Schweiker, Inc.
310 North Mayfield (5900 W). Map 1.

An interesting small church in the modern manner, it is marked by direct and effective use of brick, variety in the windows, and agreeable spaciousness in the interior. It was enlarged in 1956 by the addition of the northern part, by architect William Fyfe, an apprentice of Schweiker at the time of the original design.

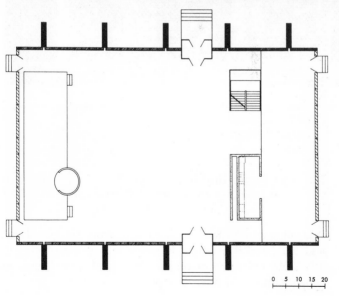

0 5 10 15 20

179

72. University Building. 1937.   L   II-B
Architects: George F. and William Keck.
5551 South University (1144 E). Map 5.

A small apartment building in modern style. The glass brick
and the external Venetian blinds seemed "modernistic" in
1937, but today the dominant effect is of quiet design in
simple forms carried out in a pleasant red brick.

FIRST FLOOR

SECOND FLOOR

THIRD FLOOR

FOURTH FLOOR

0   5   10   15   20   25   30

73. Illinois Institute of Technology Campus. 1942-58.

L   II-B

Architects: Mies van der Rohe; Friedman, Alschuler and Sincere; Holabird and Root; Pace Associates.
South State, 31st to 35th. Map 4.

Aside from the individual merit of some buildings, the campus is of great interest for the grouping of a number of structures by one of the masters of modern architecture. The buildings are related so as to suggest courts or quadrangles, but these are never completely closed, one such suggested space overlapping or opening into another, usually asymmetrically. This results in fascinating and varying visual relationships and is highly expressive of a modern ideal, the combination of freedom and order. Of particular interest among the buildings designed by Mies are the Alumni Memorial Building, 1946 (especially for the detailing, as at the corners); the Chapel, 1952; and Crown Hall, 1956. The main floor of the latter, which houses the Institute's department of architecture, is a notable expression of freedom of space.

74. Promontory Apartments. 1949. II-B
Architects: Mies van der Rohe; Pace Associates;
Holsman, Holsman and Klekamp.
5530 South Shore. Map 5.

This building is typical of the postwar trend toward simple
style, emphasis on structure, and care in planning, for both
cost and efficiency. Here light-colored brick panels and
aluminum window frames are set into a reinforced concrete
frame, the frame being emphasized by the projection of the
columns. The columns are stepped back on the outside at
the sixth, eleventh, and sixteenth stories because of the greater load on the lower parts; they are scored, but in this case
at every story, in order to soften the effect of the steps by
integrating them with a design element. The concrete is "self-
finished," not covered with some other material, thus con-
tributing to the simplicity and directness seen throughout.

185

75. 860–80 Lake Shore Drive Apartments. L   II-B
1952.
Architects: Mies van der Rohe; Pace Associates;
Holsman, Holsman, Klekamp and Taylor.
860–80 North Lake Shore. Map 2.

The citation by the Landmarks Commission reads: "In recognition of an open plan in a multi-story apartment building where the steel cage becomes expressive of the potentialities of steel and glass in architectural design." Architects admire its openness and the subtle intensification of steel-frame geometry through the vertical non-structural I-beams welded to the outside covering of the frame. An interesting refinement is found in the fact that the outer two windows in each group of four are slightly narrower than the inner two. This variation can be explained by saying that it expresses the width of the piers, which are wider than the mullions, or intermediate stiffeners of the glass, and therefore take up some of the space here. This is an acceptable explanation, but the designer of this facade, Mies van der Rohe, does not always vary windows in this way. This kind of effect is better put down simply to the creative energy of the artist, in this particular design, at this moment of his career, which no explanation can quite capture (compare No. 34). In any case, the variation adds zest and vitality to the design and reminds us that we are in the presence of architecture as art rather than mere engineering, however important the construction may have been as a basis for the design.

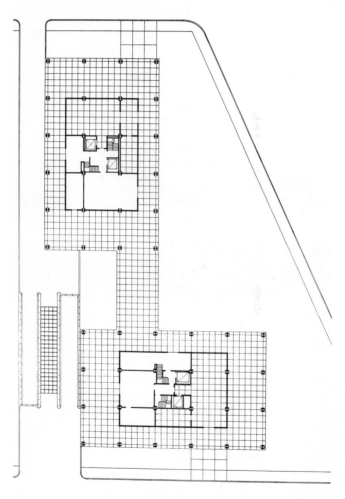

GROUND FLOOR

76. City Parking Facility ("Bird Cage"). 1954. III
Architects: Shaw, Metz and Dolio.
11 West Wacker (300 N). Map 3.

There is dramatic contrast between the closed, vertical center part, expressing the elevators, and the extremely open wings for the parked cars, the "cables" suggesting containment but with the greatest possible openness. The sculpture on the facade, "Chicago Rising from the Lake" by Milton Horn, was planned in relation to projections in the brick existing in the original design but omitted in the actual building. As it is, its sudden projection from the wall may well suggest the rapid emergence of Chicago from the planes of the lake and the prairie.

77. Chess Pavilion, Lincoln Park. 1956.   III
Architect: Morris Webster.

Lincoln Park, off the eastern end of North Avenue (1600 N). Map 2.

Reinforced concrete is used here to achieve the effect of a floating roof over a section of free space. The tables, their simplified sculpture suggesting the pieces used in the game of chess, illustrate the ideal of variety in recreation on the lake shore in good weather.

78. Lake Meadows. 1956-60.   II-B
Architects: Skidmore, Owings and Merrill.
31st to 35th and South Park (400 E). Map 4.

A contemporary answer to the need for housing in a large
city, in a redevelopment project undertaken by private capital. Various types of buildings are involved, including
apartment buildings, shopping center, school, professional
building, and recreation center, with much open and park
space provided. The apartment buildings are in the modern
manner, often with walls of glass hung like curtains several
inches outside the supports.

79. Sun-Times Building. 1957.   IV
Architects: Naess and Murphy.
North Wabash (45 E) at the River (north bank).
Map 3.

A modern newspaper plant, easily accessible to the public, where one can see the presses in operation from the hallways. The treatment of the exterior of the walls is of interest. The plaza (to the east) is not only typical of the contemporary desire to provide open spaces for pedestrians in relation to buildings in the city but is also a welcome attempt to take advantage of the inherent interest of the river.

80. Inland Steel Building. 1957.   L   II-B
Architects: Skidmore, Owings and Merrill.
30 West Monroe (100 S). Map 3.

An interesting treatment of the "wall" of a skyscraper, in that the columns are placed outside the building, as it were, the lines of the columns thus giving emphatic expression to the vertical. The large spans possible in modern steel construction allowed the architects to dispense with interior columns, so that complete freedom for the division or arrangement of the space of each floor was achieved. The citation by the Landmarks Commission reads: "In recognition of the fine open relationship of the building elements to the site; the expression of space and structure achieving clarity and lightness through stainless steel and glass." The placing of the elevators and stairs in a separate structure, to the east, contributes to the freedom of the interior in the building proper and lends interest to the exterior as a whole.

194

195

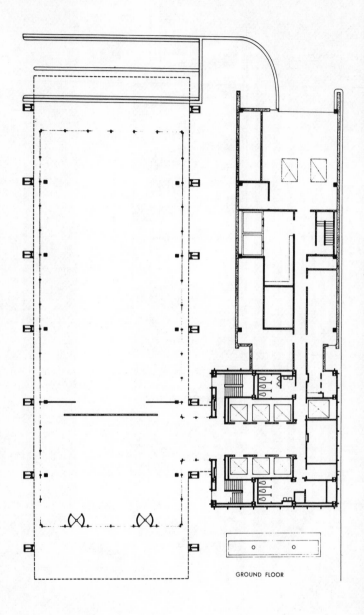

GROUND FLOOR

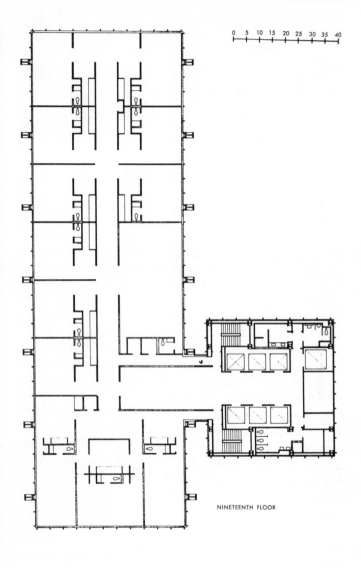

0 5 10 15 20 25 30 35 40

NINETEENTH FLOOR

81. Hyde Park Redevelopment. Begun 1959. IV
Architects: I. M. Pei; Harry Weese; Loewenberg and Loewenberg.
55th and South Lake Park (1700 E), and area to the west. Map 5.

Of interest to city planners as the largest urban renewal project of its kind when it was begun; for its emphasis on renewal rather than clearance (only 20 per cent of the buildings were to be razed); and as an experiment in large-scale co-operation of governmental, educational, and citizens' agencies (citizens' block committees originated here).

The architecture is simple in style but agreeable. One wonders, however, at the placing of the two ten-story apartment buildings at 55th Street, between Dorchester (1400 E) and Harper (1550 E), in the midst of the traffic. Their reinforced concrete is left natural, at least above the first story, and, as a result of setting the window glass at the inner side of the concrete frame, the windows create a vigorous rhythm by their close-packed ranks. The two-story town houses, of brick, have an effective alternation of wall and window in the design of their fronts, and a pleasant air of domesticity is achieved in the small semiprivate yards or terraces at the rear. The mall, in the shopping center to the east of these buildings, is also worth noting. Part of it is open, part "roofed" yet with glimpses of sky seen through openings which also allow air to circulate. It thus contributes to the character of pleasant urban living which marks the entire development.

198

82. Law School, University of Chicago. 1960.   III
Architect: Eero Saarinen.
1121 East 60th. Map 5.

The plan is wide-spreading and leisurely, with spacious corridors connecting a completely closed auditorium at the east, with lecture rooms and lounges spreading to the west. Near the center is the dramatic library, with gray-tinted glass walls which advance and recede in orderly angles, and panels which have the elegance of fine automobile bodies. A look at the stairways inside is worthwhile; they have the openness often found in modern architecture, but the treads are more massive than usual, the combination achieving a quite individual character.

The abstract sculpture in the pool on the north was made by Antoine Pevsner especially for this building and is called "Construction in Space in the Third and Fourth Dimensions." The fourth dimension, time, is present only in the changing light and shadow—as in any static sculpture. This factor, however, is especially effective here, because of the way in which the curving surfaces catch the light in varying patterns.

83. McCormick Place. 1960. IV
Architects: Shaw, Metz and Associates.
Lake Front at 23rd. Map 4.

A very large building with much open space for exhibitions and conventions, including an auditorium for performances of opera or other spectacles, all in a simple modern treatment. Dining rooms on the east side feature impressive views of the lake and of Meigs Field, a small municipal airport. The western walls are largely without windows and utilize sculpture by Costantino Nivola to lend interest to their vast expanse, but the relief is so low, and so rounded, that it does not make its effect in most lights and is probably best seen when floodlighted at night.

84. Atrium Houses. 1961. III
Architect: Y. C. Wong.
1370 East Madison Park (5046 S). Map 5.

The ultimate in reticence. The houses are closed up on the outside, opening to an interior court, or "atrium." The exterior walls are of a subdued light tan brick, without decoration or relief, the headers at every sixth course making a scarcely noticeable variation. There is no cornice, only a simple beam at the top of the wall; an extremely modest doorstep leads to the tall simple door openings. Here the architecture quietly but distinctly says "Private."

85. Hartford Insurance Building. 1961.   **III**
Architects: Skidmore, Owings and Merrill.
Hartford Plaza, 100 South Wacker (360 W). Map 3.

An interesting solution in one of today's chief areas for experiment: the treatment of the "wall" of a skyscraper. Here the glass is hung back deeply within a reinforced concrete frame, providing functional advantages, such as shading the glass area and giving easier access for washing it. The primary value, however, would seem to be aesthetic —the introduction of an interesting depth into the facades, a welcome contrast to the many recent skinlike walls. The horizontal members of the concrete frame are slightly curved on their undersides, thus greatly enlivening the design. (For an early example of the enlivening effect of curves, see No. 27.) The concrete frame is surfaced in light gray granite.

86. Continental Insurance Building. 1962.   III
   Architects: C. F. Murphy Associates.
   55 East Jackson (300 S). Map 3.

A good example of the general level of design that followed
the appearance of landmarks such as the 860–80 Lake Shore
Apartments (No. 75). The wall is a clear expression of the
vertical supports and horizontal floors, and the great width
of the bays suggests the continued development of steel construction. The building recalls modern tendencies to reserve
some space around the actual structure, here at least to the
extent of a covered area like an extra sidewalk. See No. 44.

207

87. **Marina City.** 1964. IV
Architects: Bertrand Goldberg Associates.
The River (north bank) between State and
Dearborn (36 W). Map 3.

A tightly unified complex embracing apartments, garages,
restaurants, office building, bank, and marina (with a
theater to follow in the future). The group is dominated by
the two sixty-story apartment towers, extraordinary examples of concrete construction in which the loads are carried
mainly by cylindrical cores or "sheer walls." The parking
space is a helical slab rising continuously through the first
eighteen stories of each tower. By cantilevering the floors at
every room into rings of semicircular balconies, the architects transformed the smooth cylinders into lively repetitive
patterns of flowerlike shapes.

209

88. Loop Synagogue. 1963.   III
Architects: Loebl, Schlossman and Bennett.
16 South Clark (100 W). Map 3.

An interesting solution to the problem of a church on a
downtown city street. The interest is concentrated on the
interior: the seating arrangements and the placing of the
balcony are so handled as to counteract the narrow shape
imposed by the city lot, and a pleasant effect of spaciousness
results. The interior is noteworthy also for the modern
stained-glass window by American painter Abraham Rattner. The sculpture on the exterior, "Hands of Peace" by
Israeli sculptor Henri Azaz, is not so effective, being somewhat lost in the clutter of the street.

210

89. Chicago O'Hare   **IV**
International Airport. **1963.**
Architects: Naess and Murphy.
Northwest of City Limits. Map 1.

An example of the world-wide transportation terminal of the
present day: a large airport, connected with the downtown
area by a modern high-speed artery, the John F. Kennedy
(Northwest) Expressway. The large-scale planning is noteworthy, especially in the arrangement of the various termi-
nals, the fields, hangars, maintenance areas, and levels of
roadway. The spreading U-shaped supports of the latter are
very handsome pieces of engineering architecture.

90. Civic Center. 1964-65.   **IV**

*Architects: C. F. Murphy Associates; Loebl, Schloss-
man and Bennett; Skidmore, Owings and Merrill.*
Randolph, Washington, Dearborn, and Clark. Map 3.

The building is thirty-one stories high, containing court-
rooms and offices, and stands on the northern part of the
block, the rest of the block being reserved for a civic plaza
at street level. The plaza is intended to provide for civic
functions related to the city and county governments, and for
general use by the public in the downtown area. There will
be a raised platform for ceremonies or for summertime con-
certs, a pool, planting, etc. The exterior of the building is of
steel and glass, the unpainted steel with an oxidized surface
of a russet-brown color; the details of the exterior are designed to minimize the weathering effects of rain and snow.

213

91. Federal Center. 1964 (first unit). **IV**
   Architects: Mies van der Rohe; Schmidt, Garden and
   Erikson; C. F. Murphy Associates; A. Epstein and
   Sons, Inc.
   Dearborn from Adams to Jackson. Map 3.

The Federal Center, when completed, will include three buildings: the U.S. Courthouse and Office Building, a tall building of twenty-seven stories, is the first to be built; next will be an office building of over forty stories; and, finally, the Post Office, which will be a low building. (The old Post Office will be razed in the process.) A substantial amount of the area is to be devoted to open plaza, so as to open up a space in the center of the city, and the three buildings have been planned in relation to this open space. Completion of this group is a further step in the transformation of Dearborn Street into the locus of one of the most remarkable architectural displays in the modern world. There are half a dozen masterpieces of modern design ranging from the pioneer Monadnock (cater-corner from the Federal Center) north to Marina City on the River bank. The majestic Federal Center itself emerges as one of the most expressive examples of Mies van der Rohe's genius.

92. Equitable Building. 1965. IV

Architects: Skidmore, Owings and Merrill;
Alfred Shaw, Associated.

North Michigan at the River (north bank). Map 3.

Noteworthy for the collaboration of owners and architects in reserving a large area as a plaza, in a downtown commercial building, thus achieving an openness all too often lacking in skyscrapers that are built to the legal limit of the lot area. This building thus carries further the beginning suggested in certain private buildings (Nos. 79, 85) and realized more fully in some recent public buildings (Nos. 90, 91). The design is interesting in the way it explores the possibilities of the four-window scheme—the outer two windows narrower than the inner ones—which was used with such subtlety in the North Lake Shore Drive Apartments (No. 75). Here the difference in width is more obvious, and the effect thus perhaps more dramatic. A pleasant tension arises in each group of four windows from the contrast of the central pair, which are nearly square, with the outer pair, which are clearly vertical rectangles. The horizontal strip of greenish-black marble below the windows adds very different horizontal rectangles which echo the horizontals of the floors. This interesting tension, or play of shapes, helps give the building a "presence" often lacking in contemporary buildings and aided here by the warm tonality coming from the beige color of the aluminum sheathing and the light bronze-tinted glass. The projecting verticals of the exterior not only set the larger units of the design but are also used in practical ways. For instance, the "piers" between the groups of four windows, although not structural—being merely shells set outside the structural piers—carry inside them cylindrical conduits through which hot or cold air is pumped to the offices from floors housing machinery at the top and bottom of the building.

93. University of Illinois,
Chicago Campus.   1965 (first units).
Architects: Skidmore, Owings and Merrill;
C. F. Murphy Associates; A. Epstein and Sons.
Harrison (600 S) and Halsted (800 W). Map 1.

The campus will be planned around a lecture center and a great court. The lecture center will contain lecture halls in six buildings which will share a common roof. This roof will form the great court, approached by elevated express walkways connecting it with major campus buildings, and it will center on an amphitheater at the present corner of Polk Street and Blue Island Avenue. Other buildings, including a twenty-eight–story staff and administration building, a library, classroom buildings, etc., will be built in accordance with a master plan intended to solve problems of traffic flow within as well as to the campus.

Bibliography

ANDREAS, ALFRED THEODORE. *History of Chicago: From the Earliest Period to the Present Time.* 3 vols. Chicago, 1884–86.

Useful for locations and dates of many buildings constructed before 1884. Rarely indicates architect.

CONDIT, CARL W. *The Chicago School of Architecture.* Chicago: University of Chicago Press, 1964.

The definitive history of commercial and public building in the Chicago area, 1875–1925. An amplification of the author's earlier, less general work, *The Rise of the Skyscraper.*

DRURY, JOHN. *Old Chicago Houses.* Chicago: University of Chicago Press, 1941.

Information on seventy-nine houses with date, location, and a picture of each, with more information on the owners than the architecture.

GIEDION, SIGFRIED. *Space, Time and Architecture: The Growth of a New Tradition.* Cambridge, Mass.: Harvard University Press, 1954.

This modern classic, the scope of which extends far beyond architecture in Chicago, is included because of the importance of its insight into nineteenth- and twentieth-century architecture and because of the excellent section on Chicago.

GILBERT, PAUL, and BRYSON, CHARLES LEE. *Chicago and Its Makers.* Chicago: F. Mendelsohn, 1929.

Many illustrations of buildings and street scenes.

RANDALL, FRANK ALFRED. *History of the Development of Building Construction in Chicago*. Urbana: University of Illinois Press, 1949.

Probably the single most useful publication on building in an area slightly larger than "the Loop." Despite the occasional error, the information on locations, dates, architects and engineers, costs, construction details, and references to illustrations is invaluable.

TALLMADGE, THOMAS E. *Architecture in Old Chicago*. Chicago: University of Chicago Press, 1949.

Readable discourse on architecture, architects, and civic leaders.

Additional Selective Lists

ART INSTITUTE OF CHICAGO. BURNHAM LIBRARY. *Guide to Chicago and Midwestern Architecture*. 1963.

MUSCHENHEIM, ARTHUR. *A Guide to Chicago Architecture*. Chicago, 1962.

RANDALL, JOHN D. *A Guide to Significant Chicago Architecture of 1872 to 1922*. Glencoe, Ill., 1958.

Glossary

CAISSON—An air chamber, resembling a well, driven down to firm foundation material and filled with concrete.

CANTILEVERED—Built with beams projected horizontally, supported by a downward force behind a fulcrum.

CAPITAL—The element at the top of a column or of any other vertical support in a building.

CHAMFERED—With the edge where two surfaces meet in an exterior angle, reduced or rounded; beveled.

CHICAGO WINDOW—A window occupying the full width of the bay and divided into a large fixed sash flanked by a narrow movable sash at each side.

COLONNETTE—A small column, often used decoratively rather than functionally for support.

CORBEL—A supporting form for a wall, consisting of layers or levels of masonry or wood, beyond the wall surface.

CORBEL-TABLES—Successive corbels supporting a superstructure or upper moldings, beneath a spire or parapet, or below the eaves.

CORNICE—The projecting member at the top of a wall; often a decorative development of the eaves of the roof.

CUPOLA—A terminal structure, rising above a main roof.

DENTILS—A series of blocklike projections forming a molding, borrowed from the Greek Ionic style.

FACADE—The face or front of a building.

FESTOON—A decorative garland, sculptured in relief as a loop between two points.

GABLE—The upper part of a terminal wall, under the ridge of a pitched roof.

GEORGIAN—The architectural style developed during the reigns of Queen Anne and the four Georges, 1702–1830.

GOTHIC—The architecture of the thirteenth, fourteenth, and fifteenth centuries, characterized by the isolation of vertical thrusts of stone masonry, and the use of pointed arches, buttresses, and stone tracery.

HELICAL—In the form of a helix, a curve traced by a point moving in a circle as it simultaneously moves along a straight line.

MANNERIST—Elaborate, highly stylized in the manner of the sixteenth- and seventeenth-century Italian painters.

MANSARD—A roof having a shape in two planes, with the lower usually the steeper.

MASONRY—Construction using plaster, concrete, and the applying of stone, brick, tile, etc., with mortar.

MOLDING—Any interruption of the plane surface of a structure, for the purpose of effecting a transition, or for decorative effect.

MULLION—An upright division member between a series of windows or doors.

NAVE—The main portion of a church or cathedral occupied by the worshippers; excluding the transepts.

ORNAMENT—Detail applied to plain surfaces of a building, whether by sculpture, incising, painting, or any other method, for the purpose of embellishment.

PARAPET—A low retaining wall at the edge of a roof, porch, or terrace.

PIER—Any upright structure used as a principal support by itself or as part of a wall.

PILASTER—An engaged pier of shallow depth.

PILE—A column driven into the ground as part of a foundation, and consisting of wood or concrete or concrete on top of wood.

PORTICO—An entrance porch.

ROMANESQUE (OR NORMAN)—Various styles of architecture, in vogue up to the twelfth century, and based on antique Roman forms.

ROSETTE—A circular floral motif, usually carved in stone.

SPANDREL—The panel of wall between adjoining columns of a building and between the window sill above and the window head below it.

SPIRE—A tall tower roof, tapering up to a point.

STRING COURSE—A continuous horizontal band, plain or molded, on an exterior wall.

STUCCO—Plaster for exterior walls.

TERRA COTTA—Cast and fired clay bricks, usually larger and more intricately modeled than bricks.

TRANSEPT—Either of the narrow side spaces, parallel to the nave, and usually separated from it by columns, in a church of cruciform plan.

TRUSS—A combination of straight members arranged and connected so the stresses in the members, due to loads on the whole, are direct stresses; used for beam action over larger spans.

VAULTED—Roofed by arched masonry, or having the appearance of a roof of arched masonry.

WINDOW-HOODS—A molding or decorative course immediately above a window which projects outward slightly from the main wall plane.

Credits for Photographs

The photographs not credited below are by the editor. The numbers refer to pages.

Beitzell, Neil, 70, 105 top, 118 bottom, 153, 194

Byer, Don, 201

Hale, Stephen, 89, 90 bottom, 95 bottom, 188

Hedrich-Blessing, 177, 190, 198, 199, 212, 214, 218

Lazan, Stanley M., 80, 81 top, 82, 83, 173

Malloch, Roger, 157, 158, 160

Marten, Jo Anne, 57, 58, 59, 60, 76 bottom, 167, 168, 178

Moore, Dave, 63, 64, 65, 66, 74, 75, 76 bottom, 164

Nickel, Richard, 53, 72, 73, 76 top, 85, 91, 94, 98, 99, 107, 126, 129, 131, 132, 136, 140, 156, 183 bottom, 187, 206, 207

Scott, L., 110, 111, 112, 113, 163, 184

Swanberg, Lars H., 49, 50, 108, 109 bottom

Sween, James, 117, 209

Tanner, Robert, 105 bottom

Willett, Mike, 102, 103, 120, 121, 146, 147

Credits for Plans

Anderson, Duane, 77

Bennett, Richard, 161, 172

Buccola, Charles, 51, 67

Dapiran, Jack, 61, 81

Dyba, Boris, 84, 85

Hemmer, Melvin, 127, 137

Jensen, William, 133

Kelly, George, 100, 101

Loftus, Thomas, 71, 95, 165

Lorenz, Joseph, 109, 143, 152

Maas, Paul, 113, 139

Omessi, Ben, 145, 151

Pederson, Charles, 162, 179, 181

Schwartz, Ralph, 122, 169

Snead, Clark, 189, 196, 197

Soller, James, 119, 128

Stromsland, Kenneth, 148, 154, 155

Swann, David, 92

Uthe, Ronald, 159

Index of Buildings

Art Institute, 93
Atrium Houses, 202–3
Auditorium Building, 74–77

Cable Building, 128–29
Carl Schurz High School, 157–59
Carson Pirie Scott Store, 130–33
Central Cold Storage Warehouse, 55
Chapin and Gore Building, 142–43
Charnley House, 94–95
Chess Pavilion, Lincoln Park, 191
Chicago O'Hare International Airport, 211
City of Chicago Central Office Building, 167–69
City Parking Facility ("Bird Cage"), 190
Civic Center, 212–13
Clarke House, 41
Coliseum, 134–35
Continental Insurance Building, 206–7
Crown Building, 136–37

Dwight Building, 162–63

Edison Shop, 164–65
860–80 Lake Shore Drive Apartments, 186–89

Equitable Building, 216–17
E-Z Polish Building, 144–45

Federal Center, 214–15
Fine Arts Building, 56
First Congregational Church, 47
First Congregational Church of Austin. *See* Our Lady of Lebanon Church
First Infantry Armory, 78
Fisher Building, 117–19
Florence Hotel and Square, 52
Fortnightly Club, 96
423–29 South Wabash Building. *See* Giles Building
Fourth Presbyterian Church and Parish House, 166
Francis Apartments, 110–13
Francisco Terrace Apartments, 114–15

Gage Building, 124–27
Garrick Building, 98–101
Getty Tomb, 80–83
Giles Building, 48
Glessner House, 57–61
Graham Foundation for Advanced Studies in the Fine Arts. *See* Madlener House
Grand Central Station, 86–87
Grover Cleveland Elementary School, 160–61

Hammond Library, Union Theological College, 53
Hartford Insurance Building, 204–5
Heller House, 120–22
Hiram Sibley Warehouse. *See* Central Cold Storage Warehouse
Holy Family Church, 44–45
Holy Trinity Russian Orthodox Church, 141
Hung Fa Village Restaurant, 164–65
Hunter Building. *See* Liberty Mutual Life Insurance Building
Hyde Park Redevelopment, 198–99

Illinois Institute of Technology Campus, 182–84
Inland Steel Building, 194–97

Krause Music Store, 172–73

Lake Meadows, 192
Lakeside Press Building. *See* 731 South Plymouth Building
Lathrop House. *See* Fortnightly Club
Law School, University of Chicago, 200
Leiter Building I, 49–51
Leiter Building II. *See* Sears, Roebuck and Company
Liberty Mutual Life Insurance Building, 152–53
Lind Block, 42
Lithographic Technical Foundation. *See* Glessner House
Loop Synagogue, 210

McClurg Building. *See* Crown Building

McCormick Place, 201
Madlener House, 140
Magerstadt House, 146–48
Manhattan Building, 79
Marina City, 208–9
Marquette Building, 116
Merchandise Mart Plaza, 176
Meyer Building, 104–5
Monadnock Building, 89–92
Montgomery Ward and Company Warehouse, 149
Morningstar-Paisley Company. *See* Schoenhofen Brewery Building
Morris Building. *See* Leiter Building I

Nepeenauk Building. *See* Chapin and Gore Building
Newberry Library, 97
Nickerson Residence, 54

Old Chicago Stock Exchange, 107–9
131st Infantry Armory. *See* First Infantry Armory
Our Lady of Lebanon Church, 150–51

Palmolive Building, 177
Park Buildings, Fuller Park, 170
Promontory Apartments, 185

Reid, Murdoch and Company. *See* City of Chicago Traffic Court
Reliance Building, 84–85
Robie House, 154–56
Rockefeller Memorial Chapel, 175
Rookery Building, 62–67
Roosevelt University. *See* Auditorium Building

St. Gabriel's Church, 68–69
St. Ignatius High School (College), 44–45
St. Patrick's Church, 43
Schiller Building. *See* Garrick Building
Schlesinger and Mayer Store. *See* Carson Pirie Scott Store
Schoenhofen Brewery Building, 138–39
Sears, Roebuck and Company, 88
731 South Plymouth Building, 173
630 South Wabash Building. *See* Wirt Dexter Building
63 East Adams Building. *See* Chapin and Gore Building
Studebaker Building. *See* Fine Arts Building
Sullivan House, 102–3
Sun-Times Building, 193

Third Unitarian Church, 178–79
30 North LaSalle Building. *See* Old Chicago Stock Exchange

32 North State Building. *See* Reliance Building
Tribune Tower, 174
200 West Adams Building, 73
208 West Monroe Building. *See* Leiter Building I
225–29 South Wacker Building. *See* Yondorf Building
234 South Franklin Building. *See* Willoughby Building

Union Park Congregational Church. *See* First Congregational Church
Universal Foods Corporation. *See* E-Z Polish Building
University Building, 180–81
University of Illinois, Chicago Campus, 218

Water Tower, 46
Willoughby Building, 72
Wirt Dexter Building, 70–71
Wisconsin Central Station. *See* Grand Central Station
Wrigley Building, 171

Yondorf Building, 106

Index of Architects, Engineers, and Artists

Adler, Dankmar. *See* Adler and Sullivan
Adler and Sullivan, 53, 70, 74, 94, 98, 102, 104, 107–8
Atwood, Charles, 84
Azaz, Henri, 210

Beman, S. S., 52, 56, 86
Bennett, Edward H., 170
Bock, Richard, 120
Boyington, W. W., 46
Brenner, Danforth and Rockwell, 140
Buffington, Leroy S., 72
Burling, Edward, 54
Burling and Whitehouse, 54, 73
Burnham, D. H., and Company, 84, 117, 130
Burnham and Root, 62, 68, 78, 79, 89

Cobb, Henry I., 97
Coolidge and Hodgson, 93
Cram, Ralph A., 166, 175

Eckstrom, Christian A., 152
Edbrooke, George H., 55
Elmslie, George G., 130
Epstein, A., and Sons, Inc., 214, 218

Friedman, Alschuler and Sincere, 182
Frost, Charles S., 134

Frost and Granger, 134
Fyfe, William, 178

Garden, Hugh, 138
Goldberg, Bertrand, Associates, 208
Goodhue, Bertram W., 175
Graham, Anderson, Probst and White, 171, 176
Guenzel and Drummond, 150

Holabird and Roche, 116, 124, 128, 136
Holabird and Root, 130, 177, 182
Holsman, Holsman and Klekamp, 185
Holsman, Holsman, Klekamp and Taylor, 186
Hood and Howells, 174
Horn, Milton, 190
Huber, Judas, 44
Hunt, Jarvis, 174

Jenney, William L., 49, 79
Jenney and Mundie, 88

Keck, George F., 180
Keck, William, 180

Loebl, Schlossman and Bennett, 210, 212
Loewenberg and Loewenberg, 198

McKim, Mead and White, 96
MacNeil, Herman A., 116
Maher, George W., 146
Mies van der Rohe, Ludwig, 182, 185, 186, 214
Milles, Carl, 93
Murphy, C. F., Associates, 206, 212, 214, 218

Naess and Murphy, 193, 211
Nimmons, George C., 167
Nivola, Constantino, 201

Pace Associates, 182, 185, 186
Pei, I. M., 198
Perkins, Dwight H., 157, 160
Pevsner, Antoine, 200
Presto, William C., 172
Purcell, Feick and Elmslie, 164

Randall, Gordon P., 47
Rattner, Abraham, 210
Richardson, H. H., 57, 97
Root, John, 62, 84

Saarinen, Eero, 200
Schmidt, Richard E., 138, 140, 142, 149
Schmidt, Garden and Erikson, 214

Schmidt, Garden and Martin, 149, 162
Schweiker, Paul, Inc., 178
Shanklund, E. C., 134
Shanklund, R. M., 134
Shaw, Howard V., 123, 166
Shaw, Alfred, Associated, 216
Shaw, Metz and Associates, 201
Shaw, Metz and Dolio, 190
Shepley, Rutan and Coolidge, 93
Skidmore, Owings and Merrill, 192, 194, 204, 212, 216, 218
Smith, Sooy, 108
Sullivan, Louis H., 53, 73, 80, 98, 102, 107, 116, 124, 130, 141, 172. *See also* Adler and Sullivan

Van Osdel, John M., 44

Webster, Morris, 191
Weese, Harry, 198
Wheelock, Otis L., 48
Wong, Y. C., 202
Wright, Frank Lloyd, 62, 94, 102, 110, 114, 120, 144, 146, 154

Architectural Landmarks
Commission of Chicago

Richard J. Daley, *Mayor*
Augustine J. Bowe, *Chairman*
Samuel A. Lichtmann, *Vice-Chairman*
Joseph Benson, *Secretary*
Ira J. Bach, *Commissioner, Department of City Planning*
Paul M. Angle
William E. Hartmann
Barnet Hodes
Harry J. Scharres
Ruth Schoneman

Advisory Committee of Architectural
Landmarks Commission of Chicago

J. Carson Webster, *Professor of Art, Northwestern University*
Hugh Duncan, *Sociologist and Architectural Historian*
Earl Reed, *Chairman, A.I.A. Committee on Preservation of Historic Buildings*
Leo Weissenborn, *Architect*
John D. Randall, *Architect*
Ruth Schoneman, *Commission member*
Samuel A. Lichtmann, *Commission member*